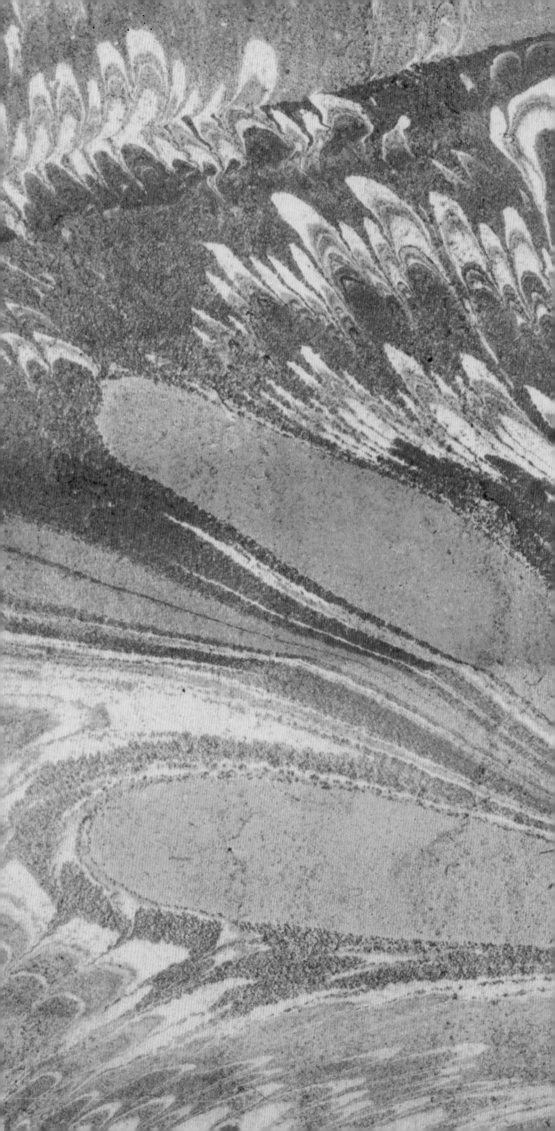

RENAISSANCE
SECRETS
RECIPES & FORMVLAS

* * * * * * *
* * * * *
* * *
*

First published by V&A Publishing, 2009

V&A Publishing
Victoria and Albert Museum
South Kensington
London SW7 2RL

Distributed in North America by Harry N. Abrams, Inc., New York

ISBN 978 1 85177 577 4
Library of Congress Control Number 2009923082

10 9 8 7 6 5 4 3 2 1
2013 2012 2011 2010 2009

Designer: Alice Clarke/Helen Senior + Associates
Copy-editor: Perilla Kinchin

New V&A photography by Christine Smith and Paul Robins, V&A Photographic Studio

Endpapers: Marbled paper from the friendship book of Wolfgang Leutkauff (see p.104)
Title page: Crimson cloth-of-gold velvet, c.1475 (see p.62).
The stars used throughout *Renaissance Secrets* are inspired by *Hypnerotomachia Poliphili*,
attributed to Francesco Colonna (Venice, 1499). *Hypnerotomachia Poliphili* is widely
considered to be one of the most beautiful books of the fifteenth century and is
renowned for its typographical design.

Printed in China

V&A Publishing
Victoria and Albert Museum
South Kensington
London SW7 2RL
www.vam.ac.uk

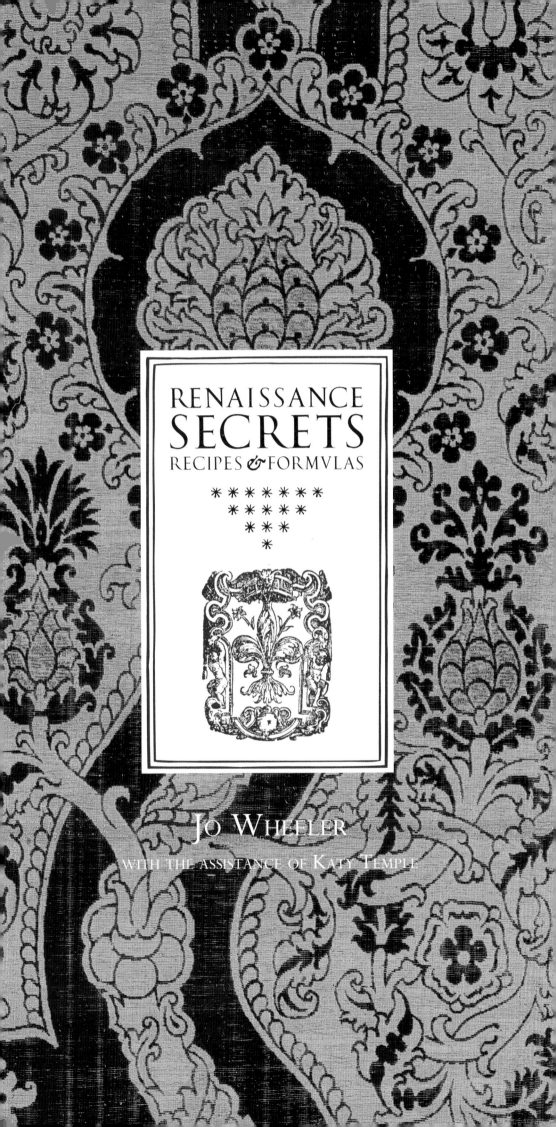

RENAISSANCE SECRETS
RECIPES & FORMVLAS

JO WHEELER

WITH THE ASSISTANCE OF KATY TEMPLE

W oodcut of a monk in a stillroom, from *Opera nuova intitolata Dificio de ricette* (Venice, 1529). The *Dificio de Ricette* (*House of Recipes*) was a short compilation of trade secrets and medical receipts, first published in 1525. Many of these recipes resurface in the best-selling *Secreti del reverendo donno Alessio Piemontese* (Venice, 1555). This image and the association of the *Secrets of Alessio Piemontese* with a supposed monk emphasize the identification of religious orders with knowledge of alchemy, distilling and other trade secrets.

Wellcome Library, London

CONTENTS

Benvenuto Cellini, *Head of Medusa*. Bronze, Florence, c.1545–50. In the famous account of the casting of the *Perseus* in his autobiography, the goldsmith, medallist and sculptor, Benvenuto Cellini (1500–71) insisted that his method 'was very different' to that employed 'by all other masters of the profession'. In reality, he relied on specialist bronze casters such as Zanobi and Alessandro Lastricati. This evidence of collaborative trade secrets contradicts the image (vigorously asserted by Cellini) of the Renaissance artist as a unique creative talent. The V&A bronze is a preparatory model for the *Perseus*.

V&A: A.14–1964

INTRODUCTION

THE TERM 'SECRET' WAS USED THROUGHOUT THE RENAISSANCE TO describe a recipe or formula. Thousands of 'books of secrets' – compilations of recipes claiming to reveal trade secrets and occult knowledge – were printed. Yet no modern book has drawn together recipes from a broad range of Renaissance trades. The carefully selected examples here cover everything from highly technical formulas for glassmaking and ceramics to recipes for perfumes, soaps and cosmetics. There is even a recipe for 'Biscuits to excite Venus'.

Every recipe is linked to the unrivalled collections of the Victoria and Albert Museum, particularly to objects displayed in the new Medieval and Renaissance Galleries or books held in the National Art Library. The recipes were selected because of their intriguing content and for the stories behind them. Many have never been studied or published before and all are based on the latest specialist research.

Were these recipes really trade secrets? Who wrote them, for whom and why? Were they for private use or intended to be published? This introduction offers some preliminary answers to these key questions, scratching the surface of a vast topic, open to much further research.

Three examples (Lustre, Venetian Scarlet and Printing Ink) demonstrate that formulas were not revealed if they were essential to an artisan's livelihood. Such trade secrets were carefully guarded. So, in early modern London, apprentices had to swear faithfully to keep their master's secrets.

The fact that many technical procedures were not written down or published as recipes does not necessarily indicate deliberate secrecy. Writing was an ineffective way of transmitting craft skills: knowledge difficult to put into words could more easily be acquired by doing. Secrets were generally passed on orally, through apprenticeships and years of hands-on experience and observation.

Take glassmaking, for example. Archduke Ferdinand II of Austria (ruler of Tyrol 1563–95) set out to create his own private glasshouse at Schloss Ambras above Innsbruck producing Venetian-style glass. In 1572, he hired Antonio Montano from Altare in Montferrato (near Genoa) where glassmakers were free to work abroad. He even arranged for Montano to visit Murano undercover as a merchant in order to steal Venetian secrets.

*Le grandi, e marauigliose virtù del dente del hipopotamo o vero del caual marino. Che
si troua nel fiume Nilo ... Dispensato da me Dionysio Alberti, etc.*, Cesare Scaccioppa
(Bologna, Macerata, Ferrara, Rome,1625). Single sheet woodcut. This handbill
promotes a unique secret 'dispensed by me Dionysio Alberti' – 'hippo tooth'. The
eye-catching image of a snarling and incredibly strange and powerful beast reinforces
the 'marvellous' and 'great' virtues of this rare cure. This secret can be seen as a
contact zone between learned and informal medicine, since hippo teeth were prized
items, displayed in cabinets of curiosities and early museums of natural history.

By permission of the British Library, London: L.23.c.7.(69.)

After two months, Montano returned with samples of glasses, soda ash and an experienced assistant. But his efforts to produce sufficiently high-quality glass failed. This case demonstrates the exceptional skills necessary to make *cristallo* and *lattimo* glass. It helps explain why the printing of numerous formulas in the glassmaking treatise *L'arte vetraria* (*The Art of Glass*) by Antonio Neri in 1612 had no discernible impact on demand for Venetian know-how across Europe (see pp.17, 19).

As courts were among the most prominent centres of practical alchemy and chemical medicine, such recipes frequently circulated in manuscript and correspondence amongst the elite. According to the Danish astronomer Tycho Brahe, 'it serves no useful purpose, and is unreasonable to make such things common knowledge'. These secrets were part of the currency of diplomacy and friendship and were frequently exchanged as gifts. For instance, Anna of Saxony, daughter of Christian III of Denmark, distributed hundreds of jars of her distilled medicinal waters each year as gifts to noble and other correspondents.

Tycho's youngest sister, Sophie, was similarly expert in preparing chemical therapies; he revealed to her the secret recipe for his famous anti-plague remedy in a coded letter to his noble kinsman Holger Rosenkrantz.

Other trade secrets though were routinely sold. Medical charlatans printed booklets of receipts and handbills, frequently retailed from public stages along with their simple remedies and products such as oils, soaps, dentifrices and scented waters. In 1614, the Roman licensing authorities in an attempt to control this trade decreed 'that no one should dare to print booklets, recipes, or sheets describing said virtues [...] unless they have been approved and undersigned by us'.

Artisans also wrote full-scale manuals, packed with detailed formulas. Italian examples include Vannoccio Biringuccio on metallurgy (Venice, 1540), Benvenuto Cellini on goldsmithing and sculpture (Florence, 1565) and Bartolomeo Scappi on cookery (Venice, 1570). Yet all these works were produced right at the very end of their careers and all were intended chiefly to educate patrons, and lend prestige to their art. Non-professionals also produced comprehensive manuals: Antonio Neri (on glass), Cipriano Piccolpasso (on ceramics)[1] and Giovanventura Rosetti (on dyeing and perfumery). The intended audiences of Biringuccio, Cellini, Neri and Piccolpasso were not artisans. Only Scappi addressed his work to his apprentice.

Meanwhile, away from court circles, a new demand was being created not by artisans but by enterprising publishers and professional writers, feeding a burgeoning printing industry with new 'must-have' products

Gabrielle Magino, *Dialoghi … sopra l'utili sue inventioni circa la seta* (Rome, 1588), Fig. 2 (Santa Maria Maggiore with the vineyard of Sixtus V). Renaissance trades are often studied in isolation, but a single individual could traffic in secrets across several trades. Gabrielle Magino is a prime example. Here in *Dialogues on the Useful Inventions for Silk* he is shown on the right with one of his secrets for hatching silkworms twice a year, stirring the eggs in tepid malmsey wine (see p.67). In Rome alone, Magino obtained patents for distilled 'medicines from wild herbs' and for an oil to render fine crystal and vessels used in taverns more transparent.

The Bodleian Library, University of Oxford: Douce G subt. 8, p.23

aimed at an ever-broader public. In the early 1530s, four separate pamphlets of recipes became immediate bestsellers in various German towns. Christian Egenolff, a Strasbourg publisher, assembled the first from alchemical tracts and workshop notes. This he directed at jewellers and goldsmiths. The other three were also printers' compilations. By 1535, all four tracts were published together by Egenolff and by Heinrich Steiner in Augsburg as *Kunstbüchlein* (*Art/Skills Booklets*) to form an all-purpose recipe book, marketed as essential for all skilled workmen. In this way, publishers repackaged trade secrets to reach new audiences.

The emergence of professional writers for the press (*poligrafi*) in Renaissance Italy played a major role in the commercialization of secrets for general readers. These men made a living by producing vernacular texts targeted at a broad audience: prose, verse anthologies, translations, compilations and highly practical works. One such figure was Eustachio Celebrino (see p.103). His output ranged from popular poetry and prose (*novelle*), to a Turkish-Italian phrasebook and two writing-books – one on the mercantile hand (1525), the other on love-letters (1527). Celebrino alone was responsible for three books of secrets: on cosmetics (1526), on banqueting (1527) and a short general pamphlet (1527).

Another professional writer, Girolamo Ruscelli, using the pseudonym 'Alessio Piemontese', published a book of secrets in 1555 in Venice. This was an instant success. Within three years there were ten Italian editions, and French, Dutch and Latin translations (1557–9) then swept across Europe, produced by the great Antwerp firm of Christophe Plantin and the physician Johann Jacob Wecker. Astute publishers such as Lodovico Avanzo in Venice responded to this emerging market by printing new books of secrets such as Leonardo Fioravanti's *Secreti Medicinali* (1561) (see p.73) alongside others translated out of Latin with alluring new titles. By 1580, as clear evidence of a massive popular market for printed secrets, the stock of a single printer, Vincenzo Girardone in Milan, included over a thousand unbound recipes and reams of booklets of secrets.

From 1525 onwards, Italian publishers and *poligrafi* attempted to attract the widest possible range of readers for books of secrets by marketing them as 'useful, profitable and enjoyable'. They targeted both the courts and the aspiring 'middle sort' by identifying their books with 'pleasure' and 'entertainment'. Recipes were presented as 'universally necessary'. Accordingly, Timoteo Rossello[2] addressed his *Compilation of Universal Secrets* (Venice, 1559) to 'men and women of high intellect', 'physicians, all kinds of artisans' and '*virtuosi*'. The mention of artisans and women is highly significant. This book aimed to spill across barriers of status and

Gabrielle Magino, *Dialoghi ... sopra l'utili sue inventioni circa la seta* (Rome, 1588),
Fig. 8 (Residence of the Duke, Turin). Here the inventor is shown describing his secret
methods for protecting silkworms from disease and cold, recommending the use of
perfumes from scented woods and resins to reassure and comfort the silkworms.

The Bodleian Library, University of Oxford: Douce G subt. 8, p.47

gender to reach the new readers of mid-sixteenth-century Italy. Several *poligrafi* (as editors, notably Ruscelli) spearheaded a campaign in Venice in the 1540s and 1550s to publish women's writing. It was against this backdrop that the first book of secrets attributed to a woman appeared: *The Secrets of Isabella Cortese* (Venice, 1561) (see p.37).

However, it was in England that trade secrets were first seriously directed to women readers, as domestic secrets for the well-to-do household, especially the latest food fashions, starting with John Partridge's *The Treasurie of Commodious Conceits and Hidden Secrets* (London, 1573).

Print however never superseded the oral and manuscript transmission of trade secrets. Instead all three media were interdependent. European libraries are full of anonymous Renaissance manuscripts containing miscellaneous recipes for colours, varnishes, glues, inks, dyeing, gilding, cookery, cosmetics and medicine. These contain both trade and domestic secrets handed down orally alongside others copied from manuscript sources and printed books of secrets. Many formulas were taken from alchemical manuscripts – the entire tradition of Arabic texts translated into Latin and the vernacular or derived from the Franciscans John of Rupescissa (d.1366) and Ramon Lull (d.1315). In turn, compilers of printed books of secrets plundered manuscripts systematically for recipes.

Readers today will find many Renaissance recipes unfamiliar: there are no lists of ingredients or precise timings. Renaissance Europe also had a bewildering array of weights and measures, with many local variations. For example, the Venetians used four different pounds (one just for weighing gold and silver thread). A light pound[3] was made up of twelve ounces. The ounce was divided into 8 drams, equivalent to 24 scruples or 480 grains. This was used for light goods such as medicines, soap, cotton and silk.

Finally a health warning: the recipes in this book contain many highly toxic substances, and on the whole they should not be tried at home.

---

1 Piccolpasso was a humanist, surveyor, civil and military engineer, though his younger brother Fabio was the master of a maiolica workshop in Castel Durante.

2 Rossello is probably a fictional author created by the publisher and bookseller Giovanni Bariletto and/or his associates Mario Chaboga and Troiano di Navò, as is Isabella Cortese: see pp.36 and 40.

3 The light pound was equivalent to 0.301 kg , the heavy pound to 0.477 kg. In Renaissance Florence, a pound was equivalent to 0.339 kg. In England, the Troy pound containing 12 ounces used by apothecaries was equivalent to 0.373 kg.

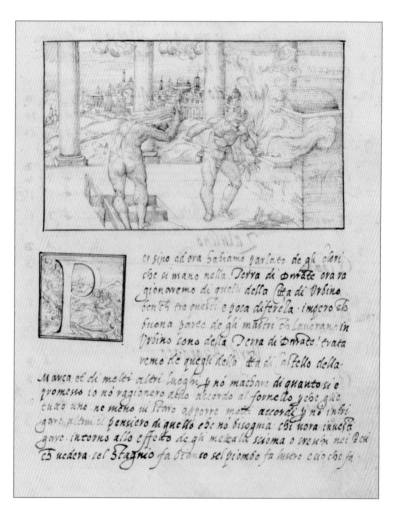

Stoking the furnace, from Cipriano Piccolpasso, *I tre libri dell'arte del vasaio* (*The Three Books of the Potter's Art*), manuscript (Castel Durante, 1556–9).

V&A/NAL: MSL/1861/7446, f.29r

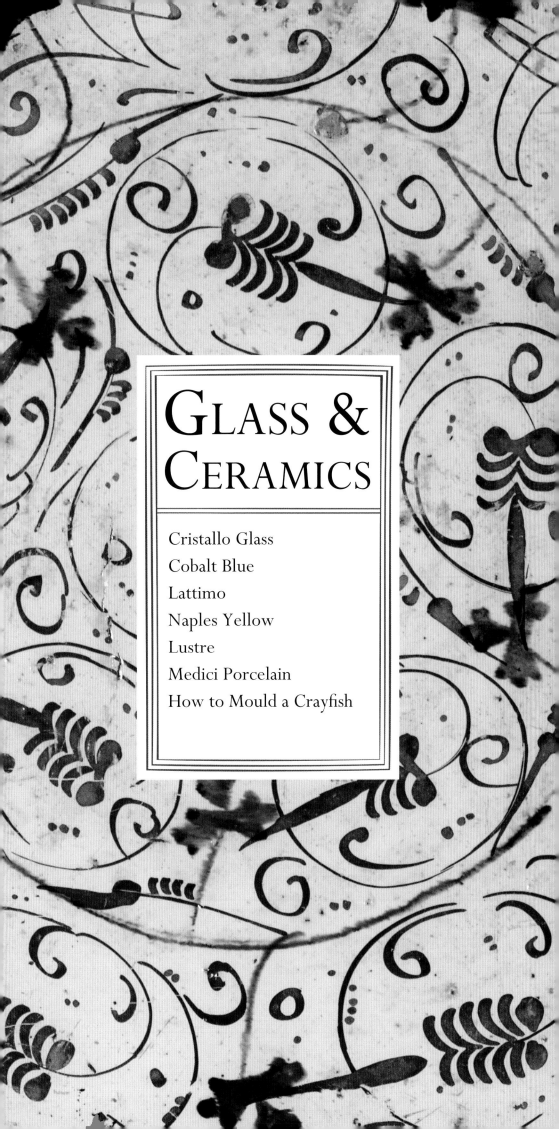

GLASS & CERAMICS

CRISTALLO GLASS

FIRST, ENSURE THE FURNACE IS SMOKE-FREE AND PRODUCING A CLEAR flame. Avoid using young and green woods. Stoke slowly and continually. Take the necessary amount of crystal glass frit and crush roughly. Place in a crucible in the furnace and leave for 12 hours. Have a tub of clean water made ready and quench the *cristallo* in it several times [...] to remove the salty deposit [excess flux] that is so harmful to *cristallo* and makes it obscure. Return to the crucible, leave to melt in the clear flames of the furnace for a maximum of four days without disturbing it at all. Add manganese at your discretion [...] and know that as all glass itself tends towards green, manganese will decolour it, but be careful to add it little by little and not add too much or the glass will turn purple. Actual practice is everything, because there are no quantities or rules. Add the manganese until the glass is limpid. Work the glass with caution, at a lower heat than for ordinary glass, above all with clear flames and without smoke, and use clean tools.

Recipe for *cristallo* from an anonymous 16th-century Venetian manuscript of glass recipes.

Private collection, f.3r, reproduced in *Ricette vetraria del Rinascimento* (Venice, 2001), p.66

Venetian glassmakers were renowned across Europe for technological innovation, above all for a new and superior type of glass, known as *cristallo*, perfected around 1450, prized for its exceptional transparency, clarity and lightness. Despite the well-known practice of craft secrecy, glass recipes did travel. As early as the 1460s, a recipe for *cristallo* was copied into a Florentine manuscript. But as know-how was difficult to put into writing, the migration of glass secrets was closely connected with the migration of workers.

The recipe to the left is particularly intriguing. It was copied almost word-for-word from an anonymous Venetian manuscript of glass recipes (illustrated opposite), dated to between 1536 and 1567. However it was written, in 1570, not by a glassmaker, but by an apothecary linked to the Medici court, Stefano Rosselli (see p.83 and 91).

The commercial value of glass secrets is evident from the repeated attempts of the Medici agent in Venice, Cosimo Bartoli, to lure skilled glassmakers to Florence. Spies were even sent to Murano. In 1569, four Venetian glassmakers leaving for Florence were intercepted by the authorities, flung into jail and condemned to the galleys. Yet by August that year, a leading master, Bortolo di Luigi Dai Tre Mori, had moved to Florence, securing a highly favourable contract, including a monopoly on crystal glass. He agreed to recruit skilled workers from Murano at his expense. And in 1574, Vincenzo Banchieri, another Medici agent in Venice, enclosed the contents page of a manuscript containing this recipe in a letter to Duke Francesco.

Several aspects of this recipe may have struck those interested in making *cristallo*. First, the directive to avoid creating a smoky reducing atmosphere in the kiln. Second, the instruction to pour and quench the frit into water, replenished until the excess flux had been skimmed off (a special process developed in Venice, known as *traghettare* or dragging). Third, the information that crystal glass was capable of being worked at a lower temperature than ordinary glass. Fourth, the instruction to add only small amounts of manganese as a decolouriser.

This recipe should not be interpreted as the workshop notes of a master glassmaker but rather as part of a basic manual probably written down for the purposes of quality control, perhaps as a framework for a *conciatore*, the worker entrusted with the preparation of the frit.

The real secret of crystal glass lay elsewhere, above all in the expertise embodied in the Venetian glassmakers themselves (regarding proportions and furnace temperatures for example) and their incredibly skilled use of high-grade raw materials – such as their purification of a special flux, *allume catina* (soda ash from maritime plants specially imported from Syria).

To prepare Zaffera that serves for many colours in glassmaking

TAKE LARGE PIECES OF ZAFFERA [COBALT OXIDE], PLACE IN AN earthenware pan and let it stand for half a day in the furnace [in the annealing chamber]. Then put into an iron ladle to be heated red-hot in the furnace. Remove while still this hot and sprinkle with strong vinegar. Then, once it is cold, grind on a porphyry stone. Wash in glazed earthenware pans, changing the water and always allowing the *zaffera* to settle to the bottom. Then decant it gently to remove the dirt and filth [...] and the good part and the tincture will remain in the bottom. Prepared and purified in this manner, it will colour much better than at first, making a clear and limpid tincture. Dry and keep in sealed vessels for your use.

✳ ✳ ✳ ✳ ✳ ✳ ✳ ✳ ✳
✳ ✳ ✳ ✳ ✳ ✳ ✳
✳ ✳ ✳
✳

Title page from Antonio Neri, *L'arte vetraria* (Florence, 1612).

V&A/NAL: 89.C.37

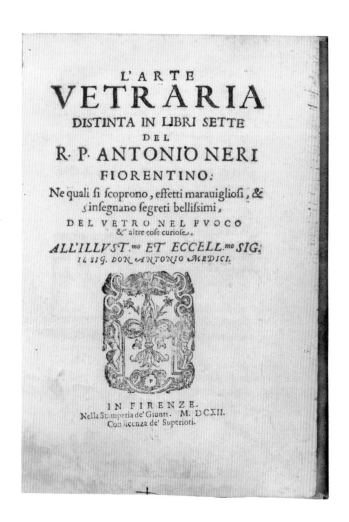

The most famous book in the history of glassmaking was published in 1612. Its author, Antonio Neri, was a 36-year-old Florentine priest and he dedicated the work to Don Antonio de' Medici, whose residence was a major research centre for alchemy and the occult sciences. In the preface to *L'arte vetraria* (*The Art of Glass*), Neri promises further volumes on his alchemical and medical experiments. But within two years he was dead. The results of Neri's search for the secret of the philosopher's stone, concealed in code in manuscript, attracted far more interest after his death than his glassmaking treatise, which only became a remarkable success much later, after its translation into English (1662) and Latin (1668).

The recipes in the *Art of Glass* are an invaluable source for revealing the production of Venetian-style glass. This is because they are based on direct observation and extensive experience. Neri worked in the Medici glasshouses at the Casino di San Marco and at Pisa (1603); based in Antwerp for the next eight years, he made chalcedony glass (simulating semi-precious stones such as chalcedony and agate) in the workshop of the Italian Filippo Ghiridolfi (1609) and experimented in producing imitations of precious stones with the alchemist Isaac Hollandus. His recipes are also highly significant because they open up the close connections between glassmaking, alchemy and the working of precious stones in the Medicean workshops. The discussion of the experimental use of rock crystal as a frit is especially revealing of the hidden collaborations behind the making of Medici porcelain (see p.27).

According to Vannoccio Biringuccio's famous treatise on metallurgy, the *Pirotechnia* (*The Art of Fire*) (1540), *zaffera* (zaffre) was prepared in Saxony by roasting raw cobaltite, ground up and mixed with sand to render it self-fluxing. 'In the company of vitreous things it becomes like water and colours them blue. Thus whoever wishes to tint glass or to paint glazed earthenware vases a blue colour uses it.' Yet cobalt blue was used by the ancient Egyptians and Romans to colour glass and by Iraqi potters to create the first blue-and-white ceramics in the ninth century. Zaffre was initially imported from Kashan in central Iran into China to colour porcelain and into Italy via Venice, where it was known as Damascus pigment. In a further example of influence from the East, around 1540 Venetian makers of maiolica added cobalt blue to create a bluish grey ground known as *berettino* to rival Iznik pottery and Ming porcelain.

Lattimo

Take 12 pounds of crystal frit and 2 pounds each of tin and lead oxide. Mix everything thoroughly with half an ounce of prepared manganese. Incorporate everything and place in a crucible in a hot furnace. Leave for 12 hours, and then stir the batch thoroughly so that the mixture fuses. If it is not sufficiently charged add further oxides, mixing well with the glass so it incorporates. After around eight hours it can be worked and you will have excellent lattimo, as I have made many times.

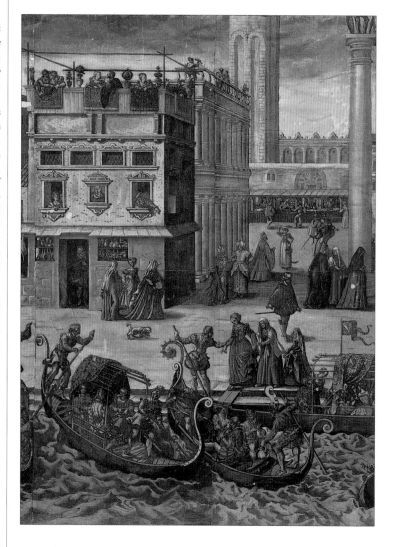

Detail from Jost Amman, *Procession of the Doge into St Mark's Square*, depicting a glass shop (ground floor window, left foreground). Woodcut in 14 blocks with transparent washes and body colours, thought to be based on a lost woodcut by Titian, *c.*1565. Only makers of crystal glass from Murano were permitted to sell crystal glass from stalls during the annual 15-day trade fair around the feast of the Ascension (illustrated by Amman).

Graphische Sammlung der Staatsgalerie, Stuttgart: inv.no A 96/6706 KK

Filigree *tazza* (wine glass) with *lattimo* glass *a fili*, Venice (Murano), 1550–1660. This elegant shape of shallow drinking glass was developed in Italy, partly to hasten oxygenation of red wine and bring out its full flavours, but could also be used to serve sweetmeats at a banquet.

V&A: 242–1853

By the second quarter of the sixteenth century, the virtuosity of Venetian glassmakers had reached a new level with the development of filigree glass, in which canes (single threads) of opaque milky-white glass (*lattimo*) were embedded into colourless *cristallo*.

Glassmakers prepared the canes in advance by stretching a gather of molten glass to form a long thread of consistent size. As it cooled rapidly, the glassmaker snapped it into short lengths. The canes were arranged inside a ceramic or metal mould or laid on a grooved flat plate, so the glassmaker could pick them up, equally spaced apart, on a gather of molten colourless glass. The canes could be kept in high relief or embedded into the gather by constant rolling on the marver (a smooth flat surface). This was one of two major techniques used.

The brothers Filippo and Bernardo Catanei, at the sign of the Siren in Murano, applied for a privilege in October 1527 to produce canes to make three types of filigree glass: *a fili* (glass with threads), *a retorti* (glass with twisted threads) and *a retixello* (net-work glass). The use of canes was certainly inspired by Venetian glassmakers attempting to imitate and surpass ancient Roman techniques, but the more complex patterns were entirely new conceptions in glassmaking.

Lattimo, which may have been developed to emulate porcelain, was first used for blown glass from around 1457. The recipe above from Antonio Neri's treatise (see p.19) is similar to early Venetian formulas except in its proportions. The incorporation of lead and tin oxides to render glass and maiolica opaque was derived from Islamic practice but was known to the Romans from the second century AD. Venetian mosaicists were using recipes for opaque white glass and enamels from the early fourteenth century. In the chapter on glass in his highly influential *The Art of Fire* (1540), Vannoccio Biringuccio noted that the white enamel ground of Renaissance maiolica was similarly composed of calcined tin and lead, underlining shared knowledge between these trades (see p.23).

NAPLES YELLOW

		A	B
ZALO (YELLOW)			
Lead	.lb	7	2
Antimony	.lb	5	2
Iron scales	.lb	3	1

		A	B
ZALULINO (PALE YELLOW)			
Lead	.lb	6	3
Antimony	.lb	4	2
Wine Lees	.oz	1	1
Common salt	.oz		½

Design drawing for oak leaf and grotesque ornament from Cipriano Piccolpasso, *I tre libri dell'arte del vasaio* (Castel Durante, 1556–9), manuscript. Another illustration from the manuscript shows maiolica painters at work with such pattern drawings or prints tacked to the wall behind them.

V&A/NAL: MSL/1861/7446, f.67r

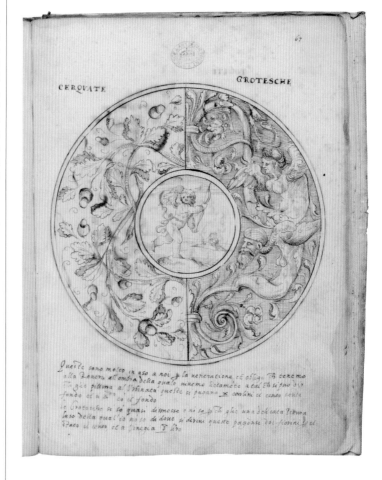

A remarkable manuscript, the earliest detailed description of the manufacture of ceramics in Europe, *I tre libri dell'arte del vasaio* (*Three Books of the Potter's Art*) by Cipriano Piccolpasso is held by the National Art Library. Written around 1557, the treatise explains the processes and methods employed in the production of Italian maiolica, the tin-glazed earthenware then becoming increasingly popular for tableware and display.

Reproduced opposite are recipes for two pigments – yellow and pale yellow – used by pottery painters from Urbino, the leading centre for *istoriato* (story painted) maiolica. They are particularly significant because these and several variants in the treatise are the first known production recipes for lead antimonate yellow (Naples Yellow). A and B give different variations of the recipe.

Piccolpasso promises to disclose 'all the secrets of the potter's art'. Whilst new research has shown this claim to be exaggerated, analysis of the manuscript has revealed an important trade secret. Many of the colours used were visible to pottery painters whilst they were working, before enamels were fired.

Glassmakers and painters used these same pigments widely. In 1541, for example, Lorenzo Lotto bought 'potter's yellow' (*zalolin da vazari*), from specialist colour suppliers in Venice at 12 *soldi* per pound.

Scientific analysis of maiolica in the V&A underlines the importance of these recipes. Lucia Burgio has identified lead antimonate yellow in the hair of one of the Three Graces on a plate lustred in the workshop of Maestro Giorgio Andreoli in 1525 (see illustration and p.25). What's more, Piccolpasso specifically recommends a mixture of lead antimonate yellows, *zalo* and *zalulino*, to simulate hair.

Piccolpasso's recipes are deliberately exact. He provides fixed rules whereas in practice the mixtures painters used were haphazard – direct comparisons between objects and pigment recipes in the treatise are thus hazardous.

LUSTRE

I PROPOSE TO GO NO FURTHER WITHOUT DISCUSSING MAIOLICA [lustreware] from what I have heard from others […] I know it is painted onto supplied pieces [i.e. those twice-fired or painted]. I have seen this at Gubbio in the house of a master Cencio of that place […] The kiln is fired and the heat gradually increased, as for other wares. The wood used should be dry willow faggots or branches, and be well seasoned. Fire for three hours with this and when the kiln visibly starts to clear, take dry and well-seasoned broom, or as Dioscorides calls it, *spartium*. Set aside the willow and heat for an hour with this. Having done this, take a sample piece from the top of the kiln with a pair of tongs.

Lustred dish, reverse (above) and front (below). Valencia, 1430–70. The galleried centre shows the coat of arms of the Florentine Degli Agli family with a lion rampant surrounded by garlic heads (*aglio* meaning garlic, a pun on the family name). These Spanish dishes with their signature bryony and parsley leaf decoration became very popular in Italy, and many survivals show the arms of distinguished Italian (mainly Tuscan) families.

V&A: C.2053–1910

The technique of applying a thin film of iridescent metallic oxides to ceramics was first developed in Iraq in the ninth century. By the early fifteenth century Valencia had overtaken Málaga as the main source of lustreware in the Mediterranean, as primacy shifted from Muslim to Christian-held Spain. Valencian lustred pottery was highly prized in Italy, not least in Florence, and commissioned in massive quantities. But around 1480, makers of maiolica in central Italy learnt this secret, adapting it to their designs.

It is clear from the Piccolpasso manuscript (see previous recipe) that this knowledge was extremely closely guarded. Even though its author had visited the Andreoli workshop in Gubbio in the 1540s, acclaimed for the beauty of its ruby-red and intense golden lustres, he reveals he had never actually seen lustre made and therefore all his information was hearsay. Even so, Piccolpasso provides two lustre recipes: one for red and one for gold. The first is a paste made up of Armenian bole, red earth, cinnabar and *ferretto* of Spain (copper sulphide); for the second, a calcined silver coin was added. All these ingredients, dissolved or dispersed in vinegar, were then applied onto twice-fired and painted maiolica. The latest technical analysis however suggests that the Andreoli family firm may have intentionally added bismuth to their secret and experimental recipes.

In the passage opposite, Piccolpasso describes how the vessel was placed in a special muffle kiln and fired at low temperature (to around 600°C). Towards the final hour, the fuel was changed from soft woods to broom, in order to produce a dense smoke and create a reducing atmosphere in the kiln. In these conditions, carbon monoxide combined with the metallic oxides, breaking them down and releasing an iridescent deposit so thin it literally shone like gold when polished.

The caption for the illustration:

Removal of a trial piece with tongs, and smoke billowing out of the kiln as broom is added. Cipriano Piccolpasso, *I tre libri dell'arte del vasaio* (Castel Durante, 1556–9).

V&A/NAL:
MSL/1861/7446, f.49v

MEDICI PORCELAIN

Transparent lead glaze or varnish

TAKE 15 POUNDS EACH OF THE WHITEST GLASSMAKERS' SAND AND select the thickest calcined wine lees available; 7 pounds of salt from Volterra and 10 pounds of golden litharge [lead oxide coloured red by mixture with red lead]. Mix everything together and sieve finely. Place in earthenware quart pots [smeared inside with fine white clay] [...] Then place in the kiln in the same manner as previously described [to make the porcelain body]. If it does not come out free of impurities, return to the kiln until fully purified. Then break the pots, remove all the clay, sift and grind thoroughly in a mill, adding clear water. Strain and sieve into a thoroughly clean earthenware vessel. Leave to rest for two days so it becomes clear: change the water, and use as needed:

Medici porcelain pilgrim flask. Soft-paste porcelain with cobalt underglaze, Florence, c.1580. The grotesque decoration, complete with mask handles, reveals the influence of contemporary Italian design.

V&A: C.2301–1910

With no expense spared, small porcelain admission tickets were issued to those invited to the magnificent evening entertainments at the Pitti Palace for the Medici wedding of 1589. They advertised the family's effort to imitate Chinese porcelain and Islamic fritware, regarded as objects of wonder by Renaissance rulers. Early experiments were undertaken at the Casino di San Marco under Francesco I, where the Grand Duke conducted research on an industrial scale into alchemy and distillation, assembling a workforce of all the talents including state-sponsored master goldsmiths, glassmakers, rock-crystal carvers and maiolica experts.

Travellers' reports that reached Europe about the formula of Chinese hard-paste porcelain, a mixture of kaolin and *petunse* (china-stone), led even hugely learned scholars such as Joseph Scaliger (1540–1609) to labour under the misapprehension that porcelain was made from crushed shells. The Medici instead believed the secret of porcelain could be uncovered through alchemical experiments, drawing on Near-Eastern expertise, maiolica and glassmaking techniques. In 1575, the Venetian ambassador recorded that Duke Francesco had 'found the way of making Indian porcelain' after ten years of trials, through the aid of a mysterious Levantine. Two years later, a small team of firing experts were responsible for production and further experimentation – the ceramicists Jacopo di Filippo and Pier Maria from Faenza, Giusto da Campi and the distiller/glassmaker Niccolò Sisti (see p.77). These imitations were soft-paste porcelains.

The formula opposite comes from a Florentine manuscript of diverse secrets begun in 1585, attributed to Giovan Batista Nardi, surgeon at the city's Bonifazio Hospital. It includes a section transcribed by a Doctor Jacopo Biscioni, including this recipe, copied from a manuscript of Grand Duke Francesco.

The glaze was intended to give translucency and enhance the underlying colours. These were painted onto an absorbent white enamel ground, a mixture of *marzacotto* (a sintered mixture of sand, calcined wine lees and salt) combined with oxides of tin and lead. The recipes and this system of layers were clearly derived from maiolica production in Renaissance Italy. The body was comprised of an experimental glassy frit prepared from powdered rock crystal, white sand, Faenza white earth and Vicenza clay.

The V&A has the world's largest collection of Medici porcelain (with nine pieces of around 70 known to survive). Pilgrim flasks were often given to newly weds, as when filled with good wine, they were thought to bring good fortune and prosperity.

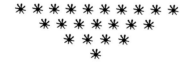

HOW TO MOULD A CRAYFISH

SO MAKE YOUR PLAQUE OF YELLOW POTTERS' CLAY, AS FOR THE other subjects. Lay your crayfish on top, upside down and with legs, stomach and eggs, which are all parts more exceptional to mould, above and on top. Push the back into the clay plaque up to almost the legs, which is about halfway [...] And so that the large legs will be lower than the head, which is sunken halfway, extend them, adding some clay underneath to raise them. Also bury the horns in the clay under the large legs so that you can position them as you please. As for the small legs, stretch them out on the clay as far as the joint.

Crayfish. The naturalist Ulisse Aldrovandi (1522–1605) amassed an immense collection of 4,454 drawers of specimens. As part of a massively expensive project of documentation and classification, he commissioned volumes containing around 8000 illustrations from nature in tempera, bodycolour and watercolour. Artists such as Giovanni di Neri (active 1558–90) and Cornelius Schmidt, from Frankfurt, employed from 1590 to 1595–6, produced these images (including the crayfish opposite). Aldrovandi managed to publish only a fraction of these drawings in his lifetime.

Fondo Ulisse Aldrovandi, University of Bologna: *Tavole*, Vol. 006–2 Animali, f.30r Biblioteca Universitaria di Bologna. Diritti di riproduzione. Bologna. Diritti di riproduzione

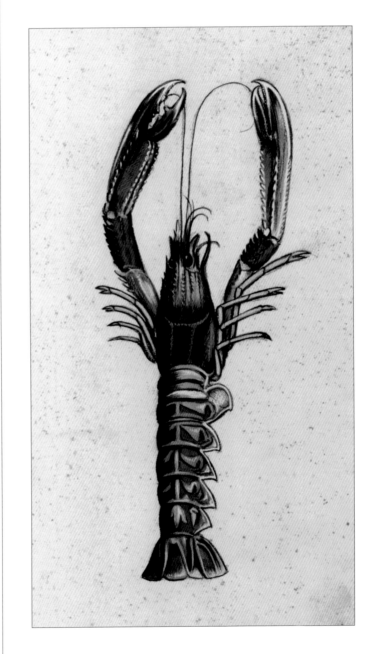

Bernard Palissy (1510–90) gained renown for his rustic ceramics: basins, ewers and dishes incorporating life-casts of animals and plants, coloured with vivid enamel glazes (illustrated). However, he never revealed any of his trade secrets. Life casting was a technique requiring prodigious skill, mastered by a few specialists including Matthias Zündt, assistant to the great Nuremberg goldsmith, Wenzel Jamnitzer (1508–85). His speciality was life-casts of lizards, fish, snakes, crayfish, and foliage. The recipe opposite is the closest known approximation to Palissy's techniques, taken from an anonymous goldsmith's treatise dating from around 1570–94. It describes the careful posing of the crayfish, capturing its motion as faithfully to nature as possible.

Palissy recounts an all-consuming obsession with the secrets of glazes in his *Discours admirables* (*Admirable Discourses*) (Paris, 1580). He presents this search as a lonely struggle in which he endured failure after failure, near ruin, exhaustion and mental anguish. The account echoes the circumstances of writing: family breakdown and his struggle to escape religious persecution. As a staunch Huguenot, Palissy was forced to flee Paris for Sédan after the St Bartholomew's Day Massacre (1572). Sadly, he ended up imprisoned for his beliefs, dying of 'misery, need and neglect' in the Bastille.

The *Admirable Discourses* (originally written as a lecture series) are a dialogue between Theory and Practice (the personification who represents Palissy's views). So when Theory asks for the formula for his glazes, Practice explains that such information is totally inadequate. The right proportions can only be learnt through trial and error. A thousand reams of paper would be insufficient to write down all the accidents that happened to him in learning this art. 'However intelligent you may be, you will still make a thousand mistakes.' Knowledge based on experience was therefore superior. But Practice also defends ceramics from the accusation that it was a lowly mechanical art. The regulation of firing required a 'careful philosophy' that tested even the finest minds, whilst a 'singular geometry' governed the arrangement of pieces in the kiln.

Practice also explains that artisans should not disclose their secrets too cheaply. Those who did so, like the makers of enamelled buttons, found themselves rapidly despised. Their buttons once sold for three francs a dozen. Now a dozen could be had for just a sou. Yet Practice says he would not hesitate to teach his secrets to Theory if he would guard them preciously.

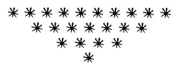

Woman bleaching her hair, from Cesare Vecellio, *Habiti antichi, et moderni di tutto il mondo* (*Ancient and Modern Costumes from all over the World*) (Venice, 1598). This practice is described by the English traveller, Thomas Coryate in 1608: 'All the women of Venice every Saturday in the afternoone doe use to annoint their hair with oyle, to the end to make it look faire that is whitish. First they put on a readen [straw] hat, without any crowne at all […] then they sit in some sun-shining place […] where having a looking-glass before them they sophisticate and dye their haire with the foresaid drugs.' Note the double comb and pots of ointment at her feet. Similar images are contained in the first 1590 edition of this famous costume book and in that by Pietro Bertelli, *Diversaru[m] nationum habitus* (*The Clothes of Different Nations*) (Venice, 1589). Print dealers and stationers did a brisk business selling such images to visitors to the city along with other miniatures for their personal albums.

V&A/NAL: 80.C.30, c.112v

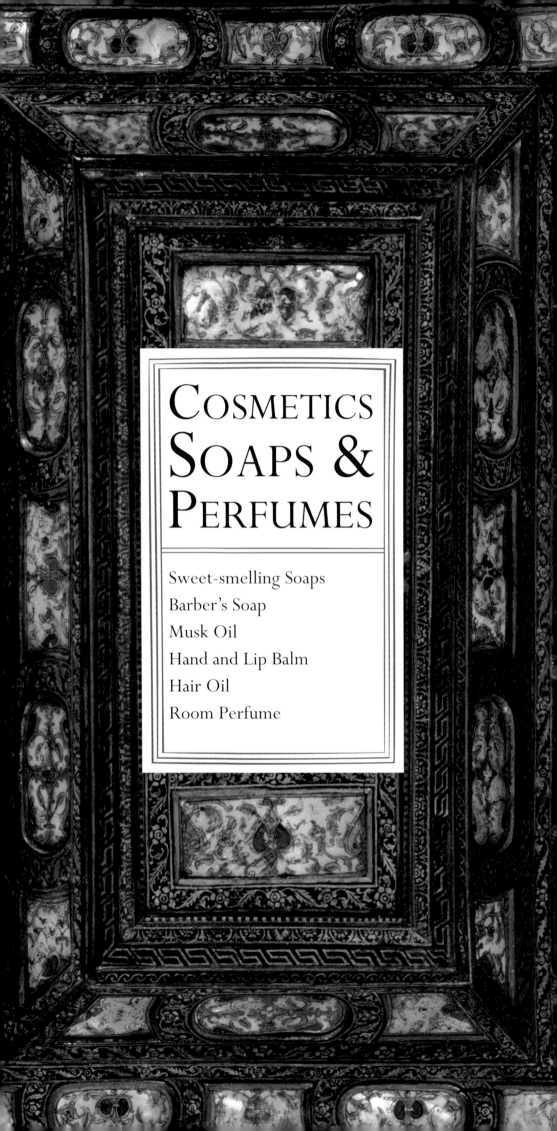

Cosmetics Soaps & Perfumes

Sweet-smelling Soaps

Barber's Soap

Musk Oil

Hand and Lip Balm

Hair Oil

Room Perfume

Sweet-smelling Soaps

TAKE A POUND OF WHITE SOAP, THE OLDER THE BETTER. CUT VERY fine, put in a basin and splash with rosewater. Mix and incorporate well. Then set in the sun, steeped in the rosewater for two weeks, and mix every day. Ten days in the sun will suffice in July or August. Mix and sprinkle with rosewater until the soap is thoroughly purged and loses its foul smell. Next take half an ounce of mahaleb [kernels of the cherry *Prunus mahaleb*] and make sure it is ground to a fine powder. Sprinkle with a little rosewater in a mortar until immersed. Add half an ounce of liquid storax [balsam from the bark of *Liquidambar orientalis*], one carat of musk and six drams of spike oil. As you grind the musk, take the oil and a little rosewater and incorporate them together. Then make into little soaps using moulds or form them into little balls. Dry them in the shade, wrap in cotton and put in a box.

Title page of Giovanventura Rosetti's *Notandissimi secreti de l'arte profumatoria* (Venice, 1555). He obtained a print privilege for this work on 28 February 1548 together with his book on 'dyeing cloth and silk', the famous *Plichto*, published that year (see p.59).

V&A/NAL: 87.D.50

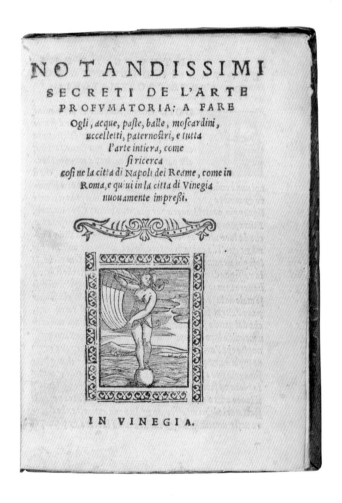

Casket. Painted
softwood with mother of
pearl plaques, containing
an interior mirror,
Venice, 1575–1600.
Scented soaps and tools
associated with the
toilette were kept in a
confanetto like this. The
popularity of the painted
and gilded moresque
designs on such boxes,
inspired by decorated
objects imported
from the Middle East,
may be related to the
exotic associations of
ingredients like musk
and ambergris in the
perfumed products.

V&A: 7901–1861

Opinion was sharply divided about recipes for cosmetics in early modern culture. In Pietro Aretino's *Dialogue in which Nanna teaches her Daughter Pippa to be a Whore* (1536) such recipes are firmly identified with prostitution. Nanna is a veteran courtesan who sets out to instruct her eager but naïve protégée in all the secrets of her art, including 'my book of recipes which will teach you how to take care of your complexion and keep your skin lovely'. Yet this can also be read as evidence of far wider practices. Women of all social levels collected beauty secrets just as they collected recipes for cookery and medicine. Throughout sixteenth-century Italy, cosmetics became increasingly accepted as outward signs of refinement, magnificence and virtuous beauty amongst the affluent and this vibrant consumer culture fuelled a growing industry.

From 1525, manuals containing tried-and-tested recipes for soaps, oils and perfumes (written by men) became available in print. But only in 1555 in Venice did the first fully comprehensive treatise appear: Giovanventura Rosetti's *Notandissimi secreti de l'arte profumatoria* (*Remarkable Secrets of the Art of Perfumery*), addressed to 'all virtuous women'. The recipe opposite is one of 18 he provides for white hand soaps.

Its most striking aspect is the great emphasis placed on the substances used to purge and scent the soap. This is because spices such as mahaleb or musk were hugely expensive commodities, costing over a hundred times as much per kilo as the finest soap. But this formula is unusual because it does not stipulate the use of high quality soap (sourced from either Venice, Damascus or Gaeta). The famed prophet Nostradamus, whose own collection of recipes was published in 1552, however advised against Gaetan soap as it 'made the hands very rough'. He offered instead his own milder 'aromatic soap', soaked overnight in good-quality rosewater, promising that after two or three uses it would make hands 'as gentle and soft' as those of a ten-year-old girl.

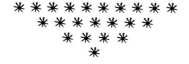

Barber's Soap

To make barber's soap at little expense

TAKE AS MUCH WHITE SOAP AS YOU LIKE AND CUT INTO SHAVINGS. Steep in rosewater. Then take powdered orris root [the root of white lily] and finely ground cloves. Incorporate all together, form into little balls and leave to dry.

Table mirror. Hardwood frame inset with mother of pearl plaques, with gilded moresque embellishments, Venice, c.1590. The relatively large size of this mirror-plate was a 16th-century development, reflecting the rising market for decorative objects associated with male and female grooming and technological advances in Venice, a city famed for its production of glass. The original plate would have been a sheet of glass backed, using mercury, with tinfoil.

V&A: 506, A&B–1897

Even lather was singled out for moral condemnation in 1583. In his *Anatomie of Abuses*, the English Puritan Phillip Stubbes attacked the barber's trade for its 'monstrous manners of cuttings, trimmings, shavings and washings'. Amongst these vices were shaving soaps, which 'bossed [adorned] the mouth' with their lather or rising foam.

The use of soaps, perfumes and cosmetics by men that so incensed Stubbes is clearly reflected in books of secrets. The formula above is from the much-reprinted *Dificio di ricette (House of Recipes)* (Venice, 1525), a text that contains several recipes explicitly directed towards men – dyes for hair and beards and remedies to combat hair loss. The intended audience of these books was therefore mixed. Women also copied down similar recipes aimed at men in their manuscript compilations, reinforcing the view that such collections were intended for family or household use. Both these cases illustrate a recurrent theme of this book – the domestication of the Renaissance, where once innovative style became part of everyday life.

This recipe is advertised as inexpensive. Although books of secrets frequently include recipes for cheap compound remedies for the poor, the marketing strategy used here appears to be one of affordable luxury, aimed at the middling sort. From other sources, we know that such soap-balls could be bought ready-made from mercers and charlatans and they were considered as gift items: Francesco Marcolini, the anonymous printer of Ruscelli's *Secreti di don Alessio Piemontese* (see p.11), sent some to his business partner, the writer Pietro Aretino (who thanked him in the same letter for also sending perfumed toothpicks).

Since medical theory recognized that aromatics were powerful therapies, it is likely that this shaving soap was thought to enliven the spirit and senses. Orris root, for example, was highly regarded as both a medicine and cosmetic. In Elizabethan England, powdered orris root was used to dust beards. Rosetti (see p.33) commends it for soaps, scented powders, to remove freckles and to whiten the hands. In books of secrets and learned medical texts, it was valued for wound care, enflamed testicles, dropsy and for teething rings for babies.

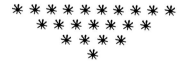

MUSK OIL

Fine musk oil

TAKE SWEET ALMONDS, BLANCH THEM USING A KNIFE AND PLACE IN A wooden box with fine musk, layer on layer. Seal the box, and leave in a dry place for two weeks or as you judge fit. Then extract the musk oil with a press […] You can give it colour with long-stalked crane's-bill. This I saw done in Rome.

To make musk oil: an excellent and beautiful thing

TAKE AS MANY SWEET ALMONDS AS YOU PLEASE, BLANCH WITH A knife or in water […] and put in a leaden box with a good amount of fine musk. Leave for six days in the musk. Then remove and grind finely in a bronze mortar. Put into a linen pouch and sew it up well. Extract the oil with a press, but first heat up the little bag with the ground almonds by the fire […] When a certain amount of oil has run out, warm up the bag again, rubbing it briskly with your hands. While still hot, press it. Repeat until you have your oil.

Recipe for musk oil from *I secreti de la Signora Isabella Cortese* (Venice, 1561).

Wellcome Library, London: 1617/A, f.80v

Musk exemplifies the vitality of trade and cultural influences between East and West during the Renaissance. Unknown to the classical world, musk (obtained from Tibet from the glands of the male musk deer) was used extensively in medieval Islam in perfumes, aphrodisiacs, foods and medicines. These uses were absorbed and adapted in Renaissance Italy along with imported musk from the Levant. Prized for its intense pungent aroma and scent-retaining properties, musk was incorporated into an array of scented products: oils, waters, soaps, powders, breath lozenges, gloves, buttons, beads, necklaces, ear-rings and rosary beads. According to the Sienese physician Pier Andrea Mattioli, musk fortified the heart, eliminated humidity in the brain and provoked sexual desire. Its use was so prevalent that when the Venetian perfumers tried to break away from the mercers' guild in 1551 they referred to themselves as *muschieri.*

The first recipe is taken from Timoteo Rossello's *Della summa de' secreti universali* (*Summary of Universal Secrets*) (Venice, 1559), a fascinating compendium of secrets that is still unstudied. Immediately preceding it is a formula for 'royal musk oil'. An almost identical variant (illustrated opposite) appears in *I secreti de la Signora Isabella Cortese* (*The Secrets of Isabella Cortese*) (see p.40). The second formula comes from Rosetti's treatise (see p.32) and was also copied with minor changes in the *Secrets of Isabella Cortese* (illustrated opposite). The close connections between these texts are rarely noticed but behind all three was a shadowy patron, Mario Chaboga, archdeacon of Ragusa (Dubrovnik), whose involvement and life remain mysterious.

In other contemporary recipes, musk was more frequently used dissolved in rosewater and in combination with two other powerful scents, ambergris and civet. The former is an ash-grey substance spewed from the intestines of sperm whales, the latter a glandular secretion of the civet cat. Like musk, they were rare, exotic and costly substances and highly valued as fixatives. Musk and ambergris continued to be held in similarly high esteem across Asia, particularly by the Mughal rulers of India.

HAND AND LIP BALM

To make a sweet smelling grease that will keep the lips and hands from chapping and make them moist and soft

TAKE 12 OUNCES OF FRESH SUET AND 6 OUNCES OF MARJORAM and pound them together. Form into balls and sprinkle with good wine. Next put into some vessel, and seal it tightly, so that the odour of the marjoram does not escape. Place in the shade for 24 hours and then put into water. Cook slowly; then strain. Take another 9 ounces of marjoram and grind up with the same suet, and form into balls; and sprinkle them again with wine. Put into another clean vessel and place in the shade for another 24 hours. Then put into water again. Repeat four or five times, always adding to them 9 ounces of marjoram and sprinkling with good wine. Finally you can add a little musk or civet to them. And you will have an excellent thing for chapped and cracked hands and lips.

Dressing case. Hardwood (probably beech), panels of painted bone, Venice, *c.*1580. This box was probably a *cassa da pettenti*, used to hold a range of implements for the toilette such as combs, brushes, scissors and glass bottles. This type of painted decoration based on Middle-Eastern designs was used for a variety of luxury objects associated with beauty rituals in late 16th-century Venice.

V&A: 217–1866

Five men gather together in Federico Luigini's *Il libro della bella donna* (*The Book of the Beautiful Woman*) (1554) to discuss 'the idea of a beautiful woman'. Their conversation is modelled on the story of Zeuxis, who when asked to paint the incomparable Helen of Troy, created a composite portrait by selecting the best features of the five most beautiful virgins of Croton. For example, the men agree that their picture-perfect woman will have coral-red or ruby coloured lips, conforming to the precepts of beauty derived from the sonnets written by Petrarch in praise of his beloved Laura. The publisher of Luigini's book was none other than Gerolamo Ruscelli, the presumed author of the hugely successful *Secreti del reverendo donno Alessio Piemontese* (*Secrets of Don Alessio Piemontese*). The recipe opposite comes from the second part of this book (1557).

The ingredients used in this balm are typical. The Sienese botanist and doctor Pier Andrea Mattioli in his very widely read commentary on Dioscorides' *De materia medica,* recommends the use of animal fats: he advises veal suet for 'cracked lips, hands and feet caused by cold' and reports a recipe for a similar salve made of suet from deer or kid with pork fat, cooked in white wine. An early sixteenth-century Bolognese collection of secrets calls for olive oil, butter and fat mixed with wax and rosewater, to which musk or civet could be added. Rubbed into the hands before bed, they would turn them as 'white as ivory'.

At least four writers who treat cosmetic recipes at length – Ruscelli, Giovanventura Rosetti, Giovanni Marinello and Leonardo Fioravanti – show a concern to provide less harmful alternatives to highly toxic substances. The use of mercuric sulphide to redden the lips was clearly widespread, recorded, for example, in domestic compilations such as those of the Bardi in Florence (see p.43) or the Nani, in Venice. These writers therefore include formulas for the lips for household use based on the dyestuffs brazilwood or *grana* (grain). They also point out the dangers of the well-known practice of painting the face with white lead. Others however chose not to – such as Giambattista Della Porta, in the expanded edition of his influential *Natural Magic* (1589).

✳ ✳ ✳ ✳ ✳ ✳ ✳ ✳ ✳
✳ ✳ ✳ ✳ ✳ ✳
✳ ✳ ✳
✳

Oil that makes hair red

TAKE 6 OUNCES OF WALNUT OIL, 3 OUNCES OF WHITE HONEY, AND 3 ounces of burnt white tartar, quenched in a glass of white wine. Leave for 24 hours so the wine absorbs the substance of the tartar. Then take the wine with the honey and put into a glazed pot with some grains of burnt cumin and the said oil. Cook until the honey burns and the wine has completely evaporated. Strain and conserve the oil in a flask. When you have your hair dressed, anoint the comb with the said oil and comb the hair in the sun and the oil will make it red.

* * * * * * * * *
* * * * * *
* * *
*

Recipe for 'oil that makes hair red' and 'lye to make hair red' from *I secreti de la Signora Isabella Cortese*, Bk 2 (Venice, 1561).

Wellcome Library, London: 1617/A, f.29v–30r

Readers of Isabella Cortese's *Secrets* (1561) were encouraged to interpret this recipe as arcane knowledge, revealed in letters only discovered after the sudden death of a travelling Viennese priest, lodging at her house at Olomouc in Moravia. It was a wonderful story, though of course fictitious, deploying a literary subterfuge common to many alchemical writings.

The use of false hair, harsh lyes and sun bleaching to produce golden hair are well-documented practices in Renaissance Italy. Less well known are formulas to turn hair red and for scented hair oils in books of secrets and medical texts.

Boxwood comb.
France, 1500s.
This ingenious comb
has a pivoted X design
construction, folding out
to form four elegantly
concave edges following
the natural contours of
the head. The teeth of
two different thicknesses
would have also teased
out dirt and lice.
A French inscription,
meaning '*I give this with
good heart*', suggests it
was given as a love token.

V&A: 236–1872

A reminder of the cultural distance between the sixteenth century and the present is that dyeing hair could be seen as a high-risk activity, as 'extremely dangerous to the head'. The physician Giovanni Marinello in his *Gli ornamenti delle donne* (*On Women's Ornaments*) (Venice, 1562) warned that this practice could excessively cool the brain, bringing on 'malignant catarrhs'. Medical opinion was divided over washing the head, as combing the hair was understood as a form of purge that removed corruption and stimulated the brain, reflecting the deep impact of the School of Salerno's thirteenth-century rules of health.

Marinello's prescription was to anoint the hair with cloves, musk and ambergris, because of their heating action. Such recipes for dyeing hair were directed towards household use, but writers were clearly concerned to influence domestic practice by supplying alternative formulas that safeguarded health.

A silver ointment jar and double-sided comb were depicted by Tintoretto in his painting *Susanna and the Elders* (1555–6); whilst Caravaggio's *Martha and Mary Magdalen* (1597–8) shows a double comb and a dish containing a sponge (known as a *sponzarol*) which were used to apply both hair oils and make-up.

What makes this recipe unusual is the lack of organic dyes recommended by other contemporary writers: alkanet or henna, recommended in Giambattista Della Porta's *Natural Magic* and the textile colorants *grana* (grain) and madder cited by Marinello (see pp. 39 and 49). The combination of burnt wine lees and oil though is an ancient one, advocated by both Pliny and Galen. The tannins in the lees would have acted as a lifting agent, removing natural colour. The oil may have been used in combination with the lye described in the recipe that follows (see illustration opposite).

Room Perfume

TAKE A POUND OF GOOD LABDANUM [GUM RESIN], ONE POUND OF ground thymiama [the dried root of *Saussurea lappa Clarke*], 6 ounces of storax calamita [resin from *Styrax officinalis*] and 2 pounds of charcoal. Place everything in a mortar and grind thoroughly together, starting with the labdanum and storax calamita. Put gum tragacanth to soak in rosewater, so they form into a paste; then add the thymiama and the charcoal. Steep with the gum tragacanth, consuming the powder and forming a good paste. Take care that the paste is not too soft or too firm, shape into *uccelletti* and dry in the shade.

Spherical perfume burner. Pierced brass, with arabesque engraving and traces of inlaid silver, probably Syria or Egypt, late 15th/early 16th century. These burners were imported to Venice from the Levant. They served as incense burners in the East, but were used as perfume burners and hand warmers in Europe. Clever suspension of the cup of burning charcoal, oil, or perhaps scented wax, on a set of gimbals inside the sphere, kept it level if hung or held.

V&A: M.58–1952

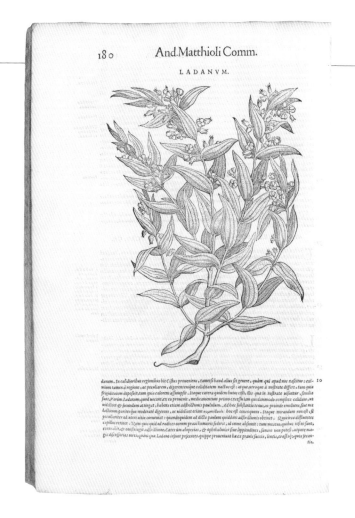

180 And.Matthioli Comm.

LADANVM.

danum. In calidioribus regionibus hic Cistus prouenicus, tametsi haud alius sit genere, quàm qui apud nos nascitur: exi- 10
mium tamen à regione, ac peculiarem, differentemque caliditatem nactus est: atque atroque à nostrate differt, tum quia
frigiditatem deposuit, tum quia calorem assumpsit. Itaque cætera quidem huius cisti, illius qua in nostrate assuetur, similia
sunt. Verùm Ladanum, quod uocant, ex eo prouenit, medicamentum primo excessu tam quodammodo complexe calidum, ut
in illicet & secundum attingat: habens etiam astrictionis paulùlum. Ad hec substantia tenuis, ac proinde emolliens, siue ma
lesciam, pariter, tum moderaté, digerens, ac uidelicet etiam superbius. hoc est consequens. Itaque mirandum non est, si
peculiarior ab ateri uitio conuenat: quandoquidem ad dicta paulùm quiddam astrictionis obtinet. Quocirca diffluentes
capillos retinet. Nam quicquid ad radices eorum praui humoris federit, id omne absumit: tum meatus, quibus insixi sunt,
conserat, & constringit astrictione. Catere ùm alopecias, & ophthalmias siue lippitudines, sanare non potest: atque ma
gis obsesuntur nocet, quam qui Ladano insunt pascentes, quippe prouenium hæc ex prauis succis, lentis, crassis, & quos secun-
tur.

Woodcut of *Ladanum* (*Labdanum*) from the translation of and commentary on Dioscorides' *De materia medica* by the Sienese physician and naturalist, Pier Andrea Mattioli, *Commentarii in sex libros Pedacii Dioscoridis* (Venice, 1565). Dioscorides was a Roman army doctor (*c.*AD 40–*c.*90) whose five-part treatise describes medicines from up to five hundred plants noting their names, their uses in treatment, how to harvest and store them, how to prepare them as drugs and possible adulterants. In 1568, Mattioli claimed sales of over 30,000 copies from the first ten editions of this work, in both Latin and Italian.

V&A/NAL: Special Collections, 87.A.31

Plague and fevers were spread, according to Renaissance medical theory, by stench. Foul vapours released from rotting material and stagnant water produced poisons in the air. Inhaling this corrupt air caused the humours to putrefy in the most susceptible. A battery of aromatic countermeasures was available to offer some protection against these deadly miasmas. By rectifying or purging the substance of the surrounding air, this room perfume would have neutralized the danger. Since smells were thought to be absorbed directly into the brain, its pleasing aromas would have also revitalized the spirits. As Nostradamus noted, nothing was 'better for protecting one against infection in times of pestilence' than the resin labdanum: 'For it cheers up humans, strengthens the heart and the brain [...] and has such a lovely perfume'.

The physician Giovanni Marinello also recommended the use of room perfumes to couples wishing to conceive a male child. During sex, the room should be filled with the heating and pleasing aromas of *uccelletti,* or musk, aloes wood, ambergris and civet. Cold or moist substances, associated with female characteristics, were to be avoided. Drinking water therefore was particularly unwise. The walls of the room should also be hung with 'masculine images', since it was believed a woman's imagination could imprint directly on the child (what she sees, she makes).

The exact meaning of *uccelletti* remains elusive, but most likely refers to pastilles shaped in moulds in the shape of tiny birds, sketched alongside a similar recipe in a sixteenth-century manuscript in the National Library in Florence. Their use is recorded as early as Boccaccio's *Decameron* (*c.*1349–51). The formula opposite comes from a manuscript book of recipes belonging to a leading Florentine family, the Bardi. Exact lines of influence are difficult to unravel but close comparison between the seven recipes for *uccelletti* in this collection and earlier sources suggests that the Bardi extracted key information from Rosetti's book (see p.33) and from an early sixteenth-century manuscript in Bologna (or a copy or earlier original) to create their own customised recipes.

Odardo Fialetti, The Painter's Studio, etching. From *Il vero modo et ordine per dissegnar tutte le parti et membra del corpo humano* (*The True Method of Drawing the Entire Human Body*) (Venice, 1608), Pl. 2. Fialetti (1573–1603), originally from Bologna, worked in Venice under Tintoretto. By 1596, he was listed as a printmaker in the city and between 1604 and 1612 he is recorded as a member of the fraternity of painters there. This work was the first step-by-step drawing manual published in Italy. This idealized etching shows the range of activities in the Venetian workshop, including the training of young apprentices, drawing from sculptural fragments or casts and the grinding of pigments. Note the depiction of verbal exchanges between master and student at centre left, vital for the learning of trade secrets.

V&A/NAL: PdP Collection

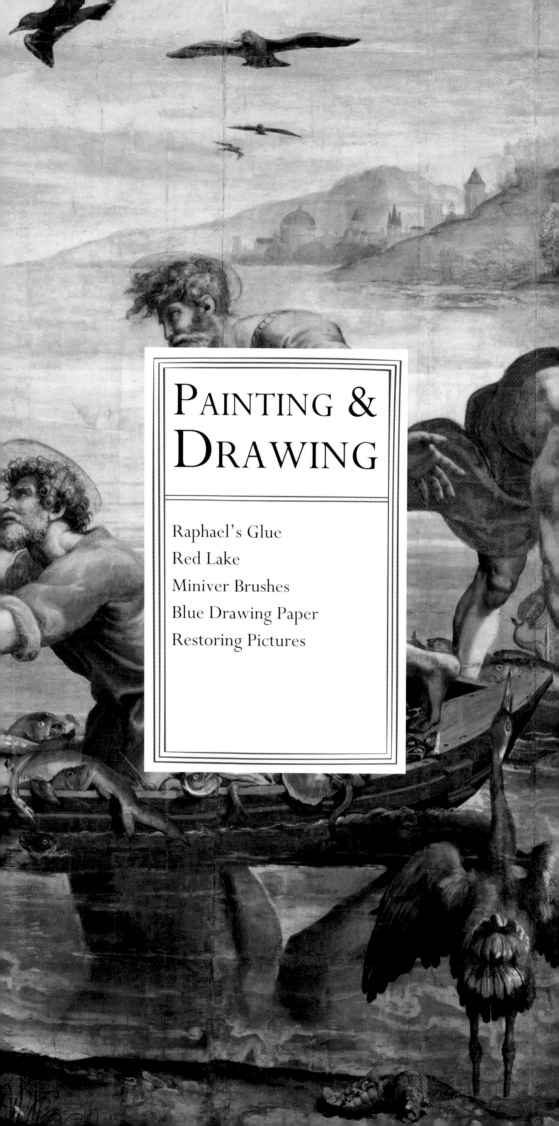

PAINTING &
DRAWING

RAPHAEL'S GLUE

THERE IS ONE SIZE THAT IS MADE OF COOKED FLOUR PASTE, GOOD for stationers and masters who make books. It is good for pasting paper sheets together and also for fastening tin to parchment. At times it is needed to paste up parchment [or paper] to make stencils. This size is made this way. Take a small pot nearly full of clear water; get it quite hot. When it comes to the boil, take some well-sifted flour. Put it in little by little, stirring constantly with a stick or spoon. Let it boil, making sure it does not become too thick. Take out and put into a bowl. Add some salt to avoid it stinking.

Raphael Sanzio, cartoon for the tapestry of *The Miraculous Draft of Fishes*. Gouache on paper, Italy, *c.*1515–16. The weavers in the Brussels workshop viewed the cartoons working from the back of the tapestries so Raphael, an experienced designer, skilfully calculated the left-to-right narrative with the gestures in reverse.

On loan to the V&A from Her Majesty The Queen

Raphael's cartoons for tapestries in the Sistine Chapel are masterpieces of the High Renaissance. Final payment was made in December 1516, and ten full-scale preparatory designs were sent to Brussels to be woven in the workshop of Pieter van Aelst. There they were sliced into one-yard wide vertical strips for use on the looms. Bought for £300 by the future Charles I for the Mortlake tapestry works, the seven surviving cartoons were still in pieces at his death, stored in 'large Deal Boxes in the Banquetting House'.

According to Vasari in his *Lives of the Artists,* cartoons for paintings were made by fastening square sheets of paper together with 'flour-and-water paste cooked on the fire. They are then attached to the wall by this paste, which is spread two fingers' breadth all around.' Raphael appears to have used flour paste glue to fasten his tapestry cartoons; though unlike both Leonardo and Michelangelo he did not hire specialist *cartolai* (papermakers) to make cartoons.

The construction of these cartoons was unusual. Each is made up of a single layer of between 180 and 200 small sheets, measuring on average 28 x 42cm. This suggests that Raphael deliberately used half sheets rather than the more common full *reale* size to strengthen the surface with more overlaps and more glue. They could therefore survive being cut up and being painted in body-colour (in contrast, cartoons for paintings were largely drawn in chalk or charcoal). Raphael's assistants were meticulous in their work: every sheet was carefully trimmed and then glued in groups of around thirty at a time rather than by rows. In all seven cartoons only one paper patch over a tiny tear has been identified.

This recipe is from the celebrated painters' manual by Cennino Cennini, *Il libro dell'arte* (*The Book of Art*), composed between 1396 and 1427, but reporting many techniques from previous generations. Another formula for this glue, provided by Leonardo Fioravanti in his *Compendio dei secreti rationali* (*Compendium of Rational Secrets*) (Venice, 1564) (see p.73), instructs that the finest-quality flour should be mixed with water and boiled with vinegar (following Pliny's *Historia naturalis*). He also recommended adding an ounce of arsenic to every pound to protect against rat damage.

RED LAKE

TAKE ONE POUND OF SHEARINGS FROM TEXTILES DYED WITH *grana* [grain, the bodies of scale insects harvested on Mediterranean oaks]. Put into very strong lye made from ashes, as dyers use, in a new glazed pot and set on the fire to boil. Boil slowly for the space of two *paternosters*. Next pass the lye and shearings through a clean linen strainer, squeezing hard so that all the lye runs out. Re-boil the lye without the shearings and when it is boiling throw in the shearings from the strainer, squeezing hard [...] Next take 5 ounces of fine powdered rock alum and add gradually to the lye until it begins to settle, which you will be able to tell as the lye will turn almost entirely to a thick scum. You must stir the lye constantly with a clean spoon until it cools and settles. Then put into a clean strainer and strain off. The lake [red pigment] will remain in the strainer [...] Leave to dry completely and put in a small earthenware basin full of cold and clear water. Stir well and rub between your fingers until it diffuses itself [...] Wash the strainer well and pour into it the water in which you dissolved the lake, and the clear water will pass out with the alum [...] When the lake is almost dry, remove from the strainer and spread on a tile with a broad knife. Leave to dry in the shade, and before it has dried out completely, cut into small pieces [...] and it is done.

✳ ✳ ✳ ✳ ✳ ✳ ✳ ✳
✳ ✳ ✳ ✳ ✳ ✳
✳ ✳ ✳
✳

Raphael Sanzio, detail of cartoon for the tapestry of *The Miraculous Draught of Fishes,* Italy, *c.*1515–16.

On loan to the V&A from Her Majesty The Queen

Pieter van Aelst, tapestry after Raphael's cartoon *The Miraculous Draught of Fishes.* Wool, silk, gold and silver, Brusssels, *c.*1519.

Pinacoteca Vaticana, Vatican
© 1990. Photo Scala, Florence

Cennino Cennini (see pp.47 and 51) saw no reason to provide a 'tedious' recipe for making vermilion. Instead he recommended that artists save time and buy the pigment ready-made from apothecaries; moreover plenty of recipes could be had from friars. The Gesuati from San Giusto alle Mura in Florence notably ran a thriving business selling high-quality colours alongside producing stained glass: Michelangelo, for example, purchased ultramarine from them in 1508. Many surviving recipes for colours occur in compilations from monasteries, and the fifteenth-century recipe above is taken from a manuscript from the convent of San Salvatore in Bologna.

The recipe describes the extraction of a red lake from the shearings or clippings of cloth dyed scarlet using a bath based on *grana* (grain). Boiling in alkali (lye) dissolved out the dyestuff; while the extract was still hot, alum was added to precipitate the pigment. Considerable skill was required, particularly in the precise strength of the lye and controlling temperatures. The formula would have produced a rich scarlet, frequently employed for translucent glaze layers. In his early career, for example, Raphael made extensive use of layered red lakes, derived from grain, madder and brazilwood.

Very few recipes survive for red lakes prepared from madder root, but technical analysis has shown that Raphael used a madder lake, probably from cloth shearings, for Christ's now white robe in the cartoon for *The Miraculous Draught of Fishes,* indicating it was originally a deep orange pink. When contrasted with the reflection of Christ's robe in the water (see illustration), painted in the more stable vermilion, this becomes even more evident.

MINIVER BRUSHES

IN THIS PROFESSION TWO SORTS OF BRUSHES ARE NEEDED: MINIVER [Siberian squirrel] brushes and hog-bristle brushes. The miniver ones are made like this. Take raw miniver tails (for only these will do) that should be cooked [...] Pull out the tip for these are the long hairs and combine the tips of several tails. Out of six or eight tips you will get a soft brush for gilding on panel, that is for wetting down [...] [Next] take the straightest and firmest hairs from the middle of the tail and little by little form into little bunches; moisten them in a glass of clear water; and press and squeeze each bunch between your fingers. Trim with scissors [...] make up the size you want your brushes: some to fit into a vulture's quill; some to fit a goose quill; others into a hen's or a dove's quill [...] Take thread or waxed silk and with two knots [...] tie each type up well, according to the size you want the brushes. Next [...] Insert these tied-up hairs into the barrel of your quill [...] Then take a little stick of maple or chestnut (or other good wood), clean it up and form into the shape of a spindle and so it fits snugly into the quill. It should be a span in length. And there you have how a miniver brush ought to be made.

Thick and fine brush and brush handle, from Cipriano Piccolpasso, *I tre libri dell'arte del vasaio*, manuscript (Castel Durante, 1556–9).

V&A/NAL: MSL/1861/7446, f.57r

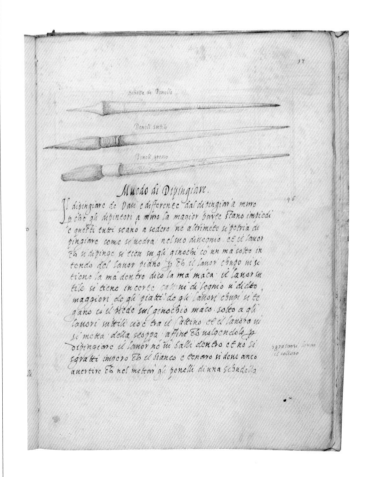

PAINTING & DRAWING

Recognized today as the most important source for artistic practice in the early Renaissance, Cennino Cennini's manual revealed Florentine secrets stretching back three generations – the techniques of his master Agnolo Gaddi, handed down from his father Taddeo, himself a pupil of Giotto. Although directed at 'anyone who wished to enter this profession', it was not widely circulated in manuscript nor printed. The likely cause is that the text was apparently commissioned by the painter's guild in Padua – so Cennini had disclosed trade secrets to outsiders.

The recipe opposite demonstrates the extent to which Cennini's work generally reflects earlier rather than current practices. In fifteenth-century Florence, most painters did not make these brushes; instead they bought them ready-made from apothecaries or specialist makers. Artists such as Lorenzo Lotto and Titian in sixteenth-century Venice purchased such brushes from the city's famed colour sellers. Accordingly, Giovan Battista Armenini's 1587 manual *De veri precetti della pittura* (*On the True Precepts of the Art of Painting*) refrained from describing how to make miniver brushes because 'they are sold everywhere in shops and by apothecaries; among the best are those which come from Venice'. Some artists though did make their own stiffer brushes of hog-bristle for fresco and other wall painting, since they were around twice the price of small fine-pointed miniver ones.

Armenini recommended miniver brushes for secco and oil painting. They were favoured by miniature painters, manuscript illuminators and for applying gold leaf. Sixteenth-century Mughal and Persian sources show that miniature painters there similarly used soft brushes made from squirrel or kitten hair, carefully graded and fastened into bird quills. As in Europe, these quills were trimmed and attached to handles of the artist's choice.

In contrast, Piccolpasso (see illustration) states that the brushes used by maiolica painters were made from either goat's hair or from the mane of an ass. For fine work these hairs were mixed with rat or mouse whiskers. The hairs were tied and then lashed directly onto sticks or wooden handles with a thread of waxed yarn.

BLUE DRAWING PAPER

Tinted paper

TAKE HALF A NUT OF TERRE VERTE, HALF AS MUCH OCHRE AND HALF again of solid lead white. Take about the size of a bean of bone meal and half as much again of vermilion. Grind well on a porphyry slab with well, spring or river water [...] Next temper with size [...] Then take a painter's pot, large enough to contain the colours you have ground and add size until the colours flow well on the brush. Take a large and soft hog-bristle brush and spread the colour with a light touch over the entire surface of the paper [...] Do this four or five times until you see the paper is evenly tinted. Let it dry before you go over it again. When finished and completely dry, take a knife and rub it lightly over the paper, removing any graininess.

How to tint paper with indigo

TAKE HALF AN OUNCE OF LEAD WHITE AND THE SIZE OF TWO BEANS of Baghdad indigo and grind well together. Temper, and use in the same manner as before.

Leonardo da Vinci recommended 'when you are well instructed in perspective and know perfectly how to draw the anatomy and forms of different objects [...] Be sure to take with you a little book with pages prepared with bone meal and with a silverpoint briefly note the movements and actions of the bystanders and their grouping [...] Its pages should be of coloured paper, so you cannot rub your sketch out.' Early in his career, Raphael followed this advice, most famously in his 'pink sketchbook' (1507–10), and – even when silverpoint was becoming increasingly outmoded as his contemporaries turned to other media – used it to sketch several figure studies for the Sistine cartoons (see p.47).

Whereas artists in Rome and Tuscany favoured cream paper and subtly coloured prepared grounds, including slate-grey, cool grey-greens and orange-pinks, in late fifteenth-century Venice artists such as Carpaccio employed a mid-blue paper to explore the play of light, using pen and wash heightened with white. This paper (*carta azzurra*) was not tinted, as described above by Cennino Cennini (see previous page), but a true coloured paper, dyed with indigo. It was originally manufactured in the Ottoman East where it was used for fine calligraphy, religious texts, marbling and even medicine wrappings. Dürer employed *carta azzurra* extensively during his second visit to Venice (1505–7) and when his stock ran out he even prepared his own version with a greenish-blue ground.

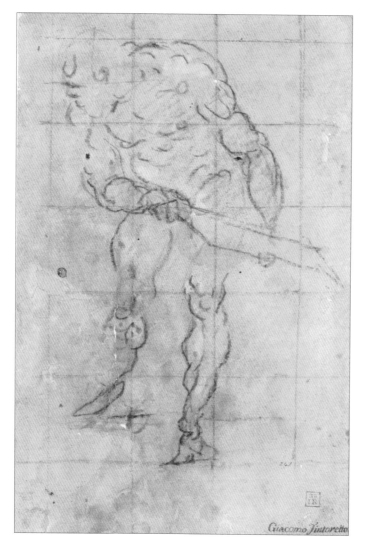

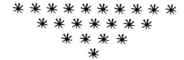

Drawing by Jacopo Tintoretto. Nude male figure turned to the left and holding an object. Black chalk with traces of white heightening on faded blue antique laid paper, squared in black chalk, 1578–80.

V&A: Dyce, 1869, inv. Dyce no.241

The finest indigo is recorded in sources from the early thirteenth century as 'Baghdad indigo' since it reached Italy from the Near East via Iraq, but traders there obtained it from Northern India (especially from Sarkhej or Biana). Lower-grade blue paper could also be produced using dyer's woad, as described in a late fifteenth-century Venetian manuscript in the British Library.

The sheet in the V&A shown here is by Tintoretto (1518–94), who consistently used the mid-tone of blue paper for his drawings, in black chalk or charcoal. This particular sheet is linked to the figure of an executioner carrying a bundle of firewood in *The Martyrdom of Saint Lawrence*. It corresponds most closely to a smaller and first version of this painting in a private collection rather than the famous painting now in Christ Church Oxford (*c*.1578–80).

Carta azzurra was not just used by artists but also in fine printing: this trend was set by the famous scholar-printer Aldus Manutius in 1514, when he produced fine presentation copies of the *Libri de re rustica* on blue paper.

✳ ✳ ✳ ✳ ✳ ✳ ✳ ✳
✳ ✳ ✳ ✳ ✳ ✳
✳ ✳ ✳
✳

RESTORING PICTURES

A strong lye that will fetch out any stain and also refresh an old oil picture and make it very fair again

TAKE ONE HANDFUL OF VINE ASHES AND THE QUANTITY OF HALF a walnut of white copperas [protosulphate of zinc] and burnt alum. Add a pint of conduit [spring] water to the said substances and strain four or five times through a hippocras bag until it [the lye] grows very strong. Set the said water on the fire and add the equivalent of one hazelnut of good soap. Heat the lye to the point that you can just bear placing your hand in it. After you have taken off the dust from the picture with some brush or foxtail, rub over the picture with a sponge until it comes to a good lustre with the said lye. And when the colours please you, wash off the said lye with fair water, and the piece or picture though never so old will become very fresh. *Quaere* [Question]: if this secret only extends to unvarnished oil pictures. Some rub over pictures or tables [panels] with an onion cut in half. This secret, with the precedent, I had of a Dutch mountebank, and they came so hardly [reluctantly] from him as if he had been extremely costive [constipated/stingy].

Jacopo Tintoretto, *Self-portrait as a Young Man*. Oil on canvas, Italy (Venice), *c.*1548. Here Tintoretto exploits oil's aptitude for giving tonal range to blacks and earthy browns, intensifying the face in contrast. During the second half of the 15th century oil painting replaced tempera in Italy as the standard medium for painting moveable panels and canvases, spearheaded by the experimentation of earlier Venetian artists.

V&A: CAI.103

'Howe to refresh the colours of olde peeces that bee wrought in oyle' from Sir Hugh Plat, *The Jewell House of Art and Nature* (London, 1594), p.51.

Sir Hugh Plat (1552–1608), lawyer and son of a wealthy London brewer, was an avid seeker of secrets. He scoured the city gathering knowledge from Londoners of all social levels, which he jotted down in pocket-sized notebooks, now in the British Library. These recipes were then rigorously tested. Those judged proven, 'perfected and polished' were published in works such as his *Jewell House of Art and Nature* (1594), intended to be of 'pleasing and profitable uses' in dire times.

Plat learnt the formula opposite to clean paintings discoloured by dirt and time from a German painter called Mr English in May 1590. Plat had already extracted recipes from him for medicines, for tricks (such as to make a man loathe the taste of wine) and for everyday problems, including how to put out a fire rapidly. Yet in print, he surprisingly disparages his informant, even referring to him as a mountebank. Plat's interest in this subject was a professional one: the latest research shows he practised the art of limning (painting on parchment, casts and cloth) and that he ran a shop in Bethnal Green, known as the Jewell House: its stock included pictures which had been cleaned and restored.

In the page reproduced above, Plat reports further techniques for restoring pictures, including the use of solvents such as warm urine, taken from his conversations with another limner, the learned preacher Stephen Bateman.

Late fifteenth-century Italian recipes similarly recommend sponging with lye and washing off immediately with water, adding that the lye must be applied with speed and dexterity to avoid removing any colours. In addition, Plat's formulas can be usefully compared with those noted in another manuscript (dated 1620–46) in the same Sloane Collection at the British Library by the Swiss Huguenot émigré Sir Theodore de Mayerne, physician to the court of James I and Charles I, supplied to him by a Flemish artist and by the royal apothecary, Louis le Myre.

Image of a Venetian courtesan, from Pietro Bertelli, *Diversarum nationum habitus* (Padua, 1594). This costume book includes a flap allowing the viewer to reveal her hidden secrets: her underclothes (male breeches) and platform shoes (*zoccoli*). Courtesans were recognised as fashion trendsetters. Costume books attempted to differentiate their dress clearly from noblewomen's, projecting a nostalgic image of a well-ordered society in which social status could be easily read through distinct clothing. Similarly erotic scenes of seduction in gondolas (with flaps) were readily available.

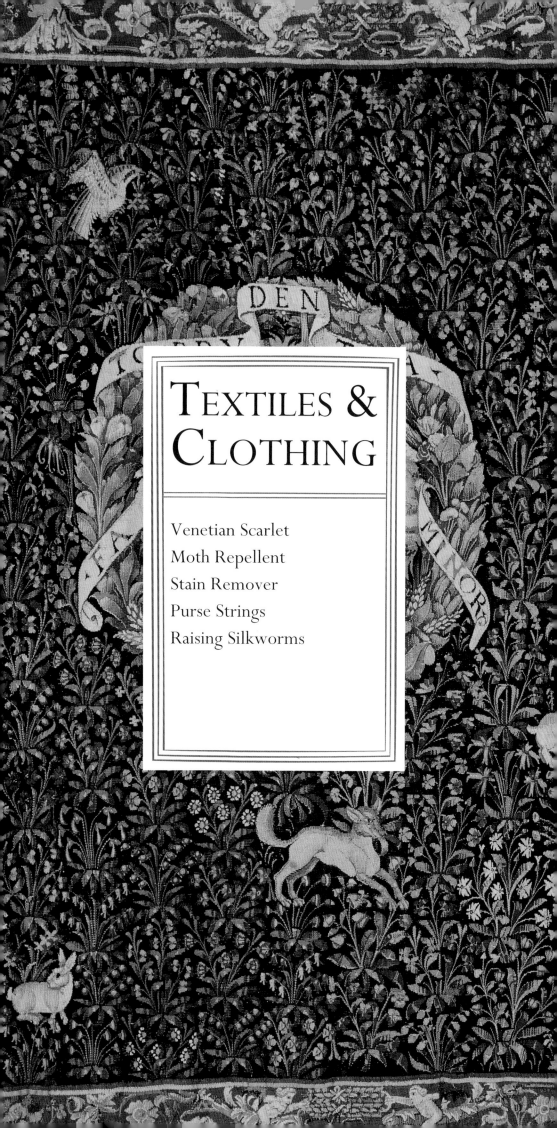

TEXTILES & CLOTHING

Venetian Scarlet

Moth Repellent

Stain Remover

Purse Strings

Raising Silkworms

Venetian Scarlet

To dye cloth a very beautiful scarlet in the manner of this city of Venice

FIRST WEIGH YOUR CLOTH AND FOR EACH POUND USE AROUND 6 ounces of grana [grain]. For mordanting, use half an ounce of rock alum and an ounce of well-ground and sifted white tartar. Take a cauldron, fill with clear water and put the alum and tartar into it. Place on a high heat and bring to a boil. Then add the cloth and boil continuously for one hour [...] Take out the cloth, and send it to be rinsed in fast running water. Wash well, prepare the full cauldron, place on the fire and see that inside are four pails of strong water [dyers' fermented bran water], thick and mordant. When it begins to show signs of boiling, put in the grain, but first ensure it has been thoroughly pounded. As it comes to a boil, put in the cloth and immerse it, plunging it beneath and give four or five turns on the bar [see illustration]. Next, remove the cloth and leave to cool. Rinse in running water. Next, prepare a new bath and give it two or three baths, with bran. Use one pound of rock alum and one pound of tartar for each bath. If the cloth is too open, give it a new bath, with one quarter of bran, no tartar and one pound of well-ground arsenic. Note that each new bath must boil for a quarter of an hour with the bran. If the cloth is overloaded, give it a new bath with bran without tartar with one pound of rock alum.

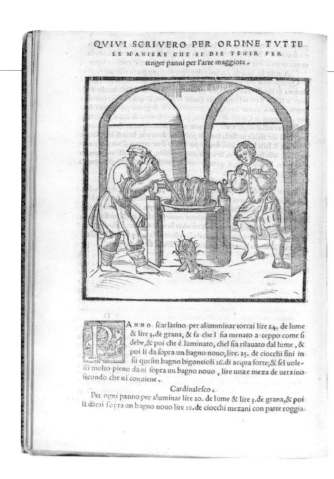

QVIVI SCRIVERO PER ORDINE TVTTE
LE M'ANIERE CHE SI DIE TENIR PER
tenger panni per l'arte maggiore.

ANNO scarlatino per alumminar tortai lire 24, de lume
& lire 3, de grana, & fa che l sia menato a ceppo come si
debe, & poi che è luminato, chel sia rilauato dal lume, &
poi li da sopra un bagno nouo, lire. 25. de ciocchi fini in
su questo bagno bigoncioli 16. di acqua forte, & sel uole-
sti molto pieno da ni sopra un bagno nouo, lire unae meza de uerzino
secondo che ui conuiene.

Cardinalesco.
Per ogni panno per aluminar lire 20. de lume & lire 3. de grana, & poi
li darai sopra un bagno nouo lire 10. de ciocchi mezani con parte roggia.

Dyers in fifteenth-century Venice naturally guarded the secrets of their art, enforcing secrecy in apprenticeship contracts, since this afforded a measure of protection against competitors. In the only surviving manual of its kind, techniques and innovations were clearly intended only for restricted circulation, since the recipes include phrases such as 'keep this to yourself, as few masters know this'. In 1548, however, a new book appeared which disclosed the dyeing formulas and processes used in Venice, Genoa, Florence and other Italian cities. Entitled the *Plichto de l'arte de tentori* (*Instructions in the Dyer's Art*), its author was Giovanventura Rosetti, who applied for exclusive rights to print this work together with his treatise revealing the secrets of perfumery (see p.33).

Venice was particularly renowned for its brilliant scarlets (luxury woollen cloths). Quality standards were safeguarded by legislation stipulating the use of pure *grana* (grain) for scarlets and prohibiting any mixtures with inferior and less costly red dyes, such as madder or brazilwood. Rosetti though does also supply recipes for half scarlets, dyed with madder without grain and 'wools of half grain', obtained with madder and grain. As noted earlier, artists used cloth shearings as a source of red lake pigments and such formulas help explain the presence of textile fibres and mixtures of dyestuffs within glazes, such as those identified in Titian's *Venus and Adonis* (c.1560). Three recipes supplied by Rosetti in his perfumery treatise provide a further example of how information from dyeing flowed across other trades. He describes how to make *pezzette di levante*, little pieces of linen dyed with brazilwood or kermes, used 'by women to rub their faces' (as rouge). Girolamo Ruscelli in his book of secrets attributed to Alessio Piemontese specifies scarlet shearings as the best source of red dye for these 'painted cloths'.

MOTH REPELLENT

How to keep garments of cloth, or hangings of tapestry, dornicks and say from eating by moths

BRUSH YOUR APPAREL WITH AN ORDINARY BRUSH AND SIMILARLY your hangings. Otherwise use a brush made from a fig frail [a basket made of rushes used to pack figs], until you have got all the dust out of them. Then brush them thoroughly two or three times a year as they hang, with a brush made of wormwood tops. To be sure, rub the reverse side with wormwood. I have heard that it is customary in summer time amongst the Italians here to hang walnut-tree leaves on threads, in such a way that none touches each other. When thoroughly dried out, they strew them in their chests and presses [linen cupboards], amongst their clothes and furniture of their chambers and beds, and between the several folds of every garment.

Moths, from a volume of drawings commissioned by the Bolognese naturalist Ulisse Aldrovandi (1522–1605), comprising 44 figures of insects, 8 of quadrupeds, 9 of fish, and 26 of shells and minerals. Aged 80, Aldrovandi published a seven-volume work, *De animalibus insectis* (*On Animal Insects*).

Fondo Aldrovandi, University of Bologna: *Tavole*, Vol. 007, Animali, f.127 Biblioteca Universitaria di Bologna. Diritti di riproduzione. Bologna. Diritti di riproduzione

Tapestry (detail). Wool and silk, Flanders, c.1540–55. This immense tapestry was woven for the Italian humanist Paolo Giovio, and once furnished the Palazzo Giovio in Como. Tapestries were usually reserved for special occasions and stored in protective canvas bags to help preserve them from damage.

V&A: 256–1895

Authors of books of secrets were acutely aware that tapestries and other hangings were extremely vulnerable to the ravages of moths. Above, Sir Hugh Plat (see p.55) in his *Jewell House of Art and Nature* advocates the use of wormwood to protect them, following ancient authorities such as Pliny and Dioscorides. A source read and heavily annotated by Plat, the *Secrets of Alexis of Piedmont*, which he nevertheless criticized for publishing untested and overly complicated recipes, reiterates this advice: 'Take wormwood, or southernwood, the leaves of a cedar tree, and valerian and lay them in your coffers or presses where your clothes be, or in the pleats of your garments.' But Ruscelli's text also provides a clear rationale for why these substances in particular were thought to be effective: 'These leaves and herbs are bitter of taste, and the savour or smell is very strong, which the vermin do abhor and cannot abide.' In Renaissance Europe, textiles were often stored in cedar or cypress chests, since the natural resins in these wood were known to be a moth repellent. Shakespeare alludes to this practice in *The Taming of the Shrew*, when Gremio mentions 'In cypress chests my arras counterpoints' (tapestry quilts).

From the last decades of the sixteenth century, new compilations of secrets appeared in England, marketed as household recipe books, with a female audience in mind. One such text was Plat's *Delightes for Ladies* (1602). The first, though, was John Partridge's *Treasurie of Commodious Conceits and Hidden Secrets* (1573). And this book includes a description of a 'fumigation for a press and clothes that no moth shall breed therein'. The recipe calls for a powder made of cypress wood, juniper, dried rosemary, storax, benzoin and cloves, combined with a powder from wormwood leaves. These ingredients were to be set on coals in a chafing dish.

STAIN REMOVER

To remove stains from scarlet or velvet without changing the colours

TAKE A HERB, CALLED *SAPONARIA* BY THE SURGEONS, *FOULLONS* IN French and soapwort in English. Heat it, extract the juice and put on the spots. Then leave to stand for one hour in summer or four hours in winter. Next, rinse the stained areas in clear water. Repeat if the stain does not appear to have gone away. If the scarlet is not dyed with grain, you may use half black soap and half juice. Mix well together and then rub well into ['frot'] the cloth and rinse in lukewarm water, and you shall see the spots cleaned forth. This is proved by experience to be true.

Crimson cloth-of-gold velvet. Italian, *c.*1475. Rich 'tissues' like this were hugely valuable, requiring highly specialized labour and expensive raw materials of silk, silver and gold. The branching pomegranate was a popular Italian design, used for noble dress fabric and furnishings.

V&A: 81A–1892

Recipes for removing stains (nos 84–7), and restoring faded colours (nos 82–3) from various fabrics including satin (no.82), wool, silk, damask (no.86) and (non-red) velvets (no.87). From *I secreti de la signora Isabella Cortese* (Venice, 1561)

By permission of the British Library, London: 1617/A, f.30v-31r

The second-hand trade was considerable during the Renaissance, with clothing and furnishings regularly rented and recycled, irrespective of social status. Also, garments were highly valued investments that precisely marked social status. No wonder then that considerable attention was paid to the care of fabrics in books of secrets, especially to removing stains and refreshing faded colours.

The first printed book containing such formulas was the *Tbouck van Wondre* (*The Book of Wonders*), published by Thomas van der Noot in Brussels in 1513. This manual was probably intended for household use, and as a result trade secrets from dyeing were marketed and sold as 'skills for everyday life'. In the early 1530s, enterprising German publishers created new compilations of craft recipes aimed at both artisans and a huge non-specialist audience. These pamphlets (known now as *Kunstbüchlein*) were a huge success, and it is estimated that tens of thousands of them circulated during the sixteenth century. Recipes, like the one above, originally from *The Book of Wonders*, then migrated into other books of secrets.

This formula resurfaces in the *Dificio di ricette* (*House of Recipes*) (Venice, 1525) and then in the second part of the *Secreti di don Alessio Piemontese* (1557). It first appeared in English in 1562 when this edition was translated. The version above comes from Leonard Mascall's *Profitable Boke* (1583), comprising recipes for removing stains, dyeing, dressing leather and for working with metals, from hardening steel to soldering on copper. All were translated from the earlier Dutch and German pamphlets. These examples alone give some idea of the extent of the rapid diffusion of such recipes for textile care across Europe. Mascall was also responsible for practical works on cattle, fishing, gardening and poultry as well as a translation of selected receipts from an apothecary's manual.

2 body's work
[requires two pairs of hands]

To make the diamond string, warp 6 boes [loops] of red and 4 of yellow and 3 boes of red on the out hand [refers to the position of the hands in a team of two workers] and 2 boes of yellow on the in hand of parties alike. And work through double boes and take all under.

2 body's work

To make the double chevron, take 5 boes of red, and give receiver [the primary team member], warp 3 boes of white and give the other party and 2 of blue, placing 3 boes on the out hand and 2 on the in hand of parties alike. And then work the Spanish breadth [flat double-width braid], the receiver taking the private stitch.

2 body's work

To make the staff and the half chevron, warp 3 boes of white and 2 of blue and give receiver, warp 5 boes of red and give the other party, placing 3 boes on the out hand and 2 on the in hand of both parties alike. And then work the Spanish breadth, the receiver taking the private stitch [but every chevron].

Purse. Embroidered paper with silver, silver-gilt thread and spangles, England, 1600–35. The drawstring braids would probably have been made as instructed above. Ornate purses like this, when containing presents such as money, perfume or jewels, would have formed part of the gift. Purses were also part of everyday dress, functioning like a pocket to hold practical items, or filled with herbs or scented powders as a 'sweet bag' to combat unpleasant smells.

V&A: T.10–1922

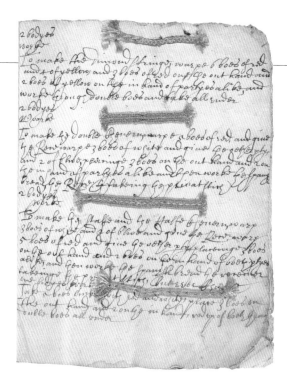

Manuscript with instructions and samples of purse strings, English, 1625–50. Some of the samples on other pages include metal thread.

V&A: T.313–1960

These descriptions for making braided strings are taken from the manuscript page shown above, dating to the second quarter of the seventeenth century. Two similar manuscripts are in the National Art Library. Another survives in the Wigan Archives, written by Cecilia, Lady Bindloss, who married in 1660. In all four, stitched above each recipe are short swatches, worked in coloured silks, corresponding to the braids (but often in non-matching colours). The Bindloss manuscript contains identical instructions to the first two sets of instructions printed here. The manuscripts assume knowledge of basic skills and standard braids.

These braids had many uses in Renaissance England. Laces (made of braid, ribbon and leather) were used as fastenings for clothes. Braids were used to dress hair, as seal tags, to trim sleeves and doublets, and as drawstrings for purses (see illustration). Notably this purse is embroidered with silver and silver-gilt thread. Decorative braids of gold and silver thread were especially prized additions to outer clothing.

The finest gold thread, made from finely beaten foil, cut into narrow strips and wound tightly around a yellow silk core, was imported from Venice and Lucca, where it was manufactured by the silk guilds. Cheaper, flexible and lightweight 'Cyprus gold' was also imported, made from gilded animal membrane. Alternatively fine silver or gold wire was made by pulling short rods through a draw plate: this was then twisted around a silk core. Silver-gilt threads could be produced by gilding silver rods prior to their being drawn into wire. In 1623 a Company of Gold and Silver Wyre-Drawers was incorporated in London, though the technique was known much earlier.

Throughout the fifteenth and sixteenth centuries, despite having no guild status, women controlled the silk industry in London. Female workers dominated the production of trimmings and haberdashery, including 'wrought silk throwen, ribans, laces and corses of silke'. They sold gold and silver thread by the ounce. The only branch of the trade in which highly skilled migrants from Italy predominated was the making of luxury cloths woven with gold and silver threads, apparently established by Milanese artisans from 1611. Also documented the same year is a Frenchwoman brought to London to teach apprentices how to make gold and silver thread, under the patronage of the Countess of Bedford.

RAISING SILKWORMS

PLACE THE SILKWORM EGGS IN A GLASS OR A TRANSPARENT AND ample vase, filled with dry malmsey or other dry strong white wine, close to a brazier to become lukewarm. Mix well with a goose-quill and leave to settle so the good eggs sink to the bottom and the useless and weak ones float to the surface. Next remove the bad eggs with the feather and throw them away [...] As well as purging the ill born so only the legitimate remain, my procedure invigorates the latter sort, so the little worms can better resist their enemies and produce stronger, purer and finer silk [...]

[To protect] against cold [...] keep the room close shut and burn aromatic woods such as pine, juniper, and rosemary or similar. Alternatively, place incense, labdanum, benzoin, storax, mastic or other sweet-smelling substances in a smokeless brazier [...] To strengthen them against cold, sprinkle with dry malmsey or other light wine. To protect from heat, sprinkle with rosewater or a little vinegar or violet-infused water, which will also defend them from disease.

Gabrielle Magino,
Dialoghi ... sopra l'utili sue inventioni circa la seta (Rome 1588).

The Bodleian Library, University of Oxford: Douce G subt. 8. Figure 5 (Venice), p.35

Jan van der Straet (Stradanus), *Vermis sericus*, engraving, published by Cornelius Galle, dated 1600.

V&A: 93.H.96

Gabrielle Magino was a young man on the make, determined to make a splash at the Italian trade fairs with the publication of his *Dialoghi ... sopra l'utili sue inventioni circa la seta* (*Dialogues on Useful Inventions for Silk*) (Rome, 1588). In this book he set out a revolutionary system for producing a second harvest of silkworms during the summer, along with 'all sorts of contrivances and instruments', newly devised by him. These trade secrets, protected by 'ample patents' covering the territories of the Papal State, Venice, Tuscany, the Kingdom of Naples, Sicily and Milan, were offered for sale along with this instruction manual. Accompanying the text were nine full-page illustrations (see opposite and pp.10 and 12) featuring the author and his inventions, with detailed captions describing the essential steps and products. But Magino failed to mention he had a business partner, a nobleman from Lucca who had settled in Venice, Giovan Battista Guidoboni, the true inventor of all these secrets. Unsurprisingly, a lawsuit soon followed and the partnership ended.

The methods for rearing silkworms described above seem outlandish but in fact Magino repeats much from the earlier treatise on sericulture, *Il Vermicello* (*The Silkworm*) (1581), by Giovanni Andrea Corsuccio. 'Long experience', Corsuccio concludes, shows that worms doused in malmsey or *vernaccia* 'become more vigorous, produce tougher cocoons, and stronger silk'. Magino lifted his detailed description of that process almost word for word, as well as his recommendation that in especially hot weather silkworms should be sprinkled with rosewater. Ironically, the real novelty of Magino's work lay solely in Guidoboni's inventions, such as the box with a perforated paper lid that protected the eggs from cold air and reduced losses (by preventing any from falling out).

Affinities with other recipes in this book can be detected in these texts. For example, the use of aromatics to combat disease has evident parallels with the uses of the same substances in room perfumes (see p.43). Interestingly, both writers also recommend laying out the eggs on *carta azzurra* rather than linen cloths, documenting another trade secret associated with blue paper (see p.53).

P eeter van der Borcht, *Charlatans*, engraving. Antwerp, 1580s. The
graphic artist Peeter van der Borcht (active in Antwerp 1572–1608)
worked as a woodcutter, art dealer, draughtsman and etcher. He was
the most productive illustrator for the great printing firm of Plantin
and his successors. Note the theatrical selling of a powerful purge
in public, the use of display posters, special packaging for the secret
remedies and what may be loose written recipes on the table.

© Rijksmuseum, Amsterdam: RP-P_A-16320

MEDICINE

MEDICINE FOR LOVERS

FOR HUSBANDS WHO HAVE HAD TOO MUCH SEX WITH THEIR WIVES, so that they weaken their bodies [...] There are many [men], indeed the majority of the young, who in the first days of marriage let themselves be so carried away by carnal pleasures that they find themselves excessively weakened, or lose their sight, memory, or other accidents befall them [...] To restore lost spirits [...] firstly it is necessary to comfort and strengthen the stomach with drinks, compresses and plasters [...] to improve the digestion. Medicines to warm the heart are also advisable; in fact they are one of the best things that can be employed [...] During this time, foods should be delicate and good; and be humid and somewhat hot [in nature]: such as chickens, partridges, capons and their broth, from which *minestra* with egg yolks, a little saffron or other aromatic and moderately hot spices is made. Avoid eating too much; and highly nutritious foods and sweet odoriferous wine are called for. Sheep's or cow's milk comfort greatly and restore the spirits, but must be taken on an empty stomach in the morning [...] white bread soaked in white wine works fast against weakness. Bathing is highly recommended, but wash your hands and feet in water, in which roses and willow leaves have been boiled. Sleep is similarly beneficial, as by extension is rest [...] a ball made from labdanum, cloves, musk, sandalwood and saffron, carried in the hand, comforts; and apothecaries have all these things.

Enamelled gold gimmel *fede* ring, Germany. Its two interlocking circles join to clasp the two hands in a widely recognized symbol of love and commitment. The joining of hands was a significant moment in the betrothal process, a tradition enduring from Roman times. Inscriptions inside these rings were common: here CLEMEN.KESSELR. DEN-25 AUG AD.1607 may commemorate the wedding date of the owner.

V&A: 854–1871

Maiolica dish. Italy, 1500–10. It depicts the handclasp, and was probably a commemorative gift, perhaps used during wedding celebrations. A pierced heart surrounded by flames was another popular design representing love.

V&A: 8900–1863

Renaissance physiology held that regular sex was beneficial to health, restoring the balance of the humours, like other forms of evacuation. Excessive sex though was both debilitating and harmful. It was most dangerous for men: according to Baldassare Castiglione's *Cortegiano,* or *Book of the Courtier* (1528), men 'dry out more than women in intercourse'. This belief rests on a cluster of ideas transmitted from antiquity, right back to Aristotle: first, that the female body was colder and wetter; secondly, that sperm was generated from excess blood remaining after the body was nourished, in conditions of great heat; thirdly, that sex for men involved a major loss of vital heat and humidity.

Alert to such dangers, the physician Giovanni Marinello (see p.43) in *Delle medicine partenenti all' infermità delle donne* (*Medicines Pertinent to Women's Illnesses*) (Venice, 1563; revised and expanded 1574), provided the sure-fire remedy opposite. Diet was central to the conservation of health, so his advice focused on eating the right nourishing foods.

The ritual exchange of gifts was central to the culture of love and marriage in the Renaissance. New brides therefore received a special power breakfast after their first night – which might include eggs for fertility and sweetmeats for love. In Florence, friends and relatives of the husband's family offered foodstuffs on the eve of the wedding and the next day brought small gifts of sweetmeats for the collation. In Rome, after the exchange of rings, gifts given to the bride by the husband's closest relatives included 'rings or other little presents'. *Fede* rings (from the Italian for 'faith', 'trust') featuring two clasped hands (illustrated opposite) were wedding rings or love tokens given as signs of everlasting love and fidelity. Also, images of pierced hearts and joined hands on maiolica plates (illustrated above) suggest their probable function as gifts to commemorate and celebrate married love.

A Charlatan's Secret

Gout is a corrupt and putrid disease [...] that is especially difficult to treat. Take around a hundred litres of sweet, young aromatic red wine and put it in a barrel that will impart a good smell and taste. Add to the wine 3 ounces of the finest ground aloes wood, 4 ounces of oak-fern [common polypody], 2 ounces of sienna from the Levant, 10 grains of musk dissolved in rosewater and 2 pounds of honey. Fully incorporate all of the aforementioned things into the wine and leave to stand for two or three days until it clears. Then it is ready to drink [...] This wine makes you shit, but if it purges excessively, hold off drinking it for two or three days. This wine will work miracles against gout and all pains caused by corruption of the humours, as it resolves, dries out and preserves the body.

This I kept secret, not wishing to reveal it to the world. But seeing that I am close to passing to another better life, I want to reveal it [...] I leave this and all my secrets, except two: my *magna medicina* and my 'great preservative' which will keep food on my table until I make my passage to another life.

Portrait of Leonardo Fioravanti from his *Tesoro della vita humana* (Venice, 1582).

By permission of the British Library, London: 1170.d.4

His strength draining, this is how the Bolognese irregular practitioner Leonardo Fioravanti (b.1517) gave up his most valuable secret. In his prime, his treatment for gout (painful inflammation in the joints linked with excessive consumption of rich foods and alcohol) was known right across Europe. In 1569, he received a letter from Knyszyn in Podlesia, annexed by the Polish crown that year. The vice-chancellor asked Fioravanti to cure his and his wife's gout. Fioravanti replied, prescribing no less than four of his own unique remedies to thin 'corrupt humours caused by indigestion', including his secret quintessence (above) and a trademark drastic purge, his 'angelic electuary'. A further three remedies were needed to keep the disease at bay.

Fioravanti's reputation was achieved through advertising his secrets in print. He went into business with a very astute publisher, Ludovico Avanzo, and with professional writers for the Venetian press, who spiced up his texts with compelling anecdotes, fables, essays, recipes written in code and sensational trade names for his drugs. On a collision course with the medical establishment, lacking both credentials and connections, he saw that marketing could provide the kind of credit and rewards he sought. So he encouraged readers to consult him directly through his publisher and to visit the few pharmacies that made up his nostrums. His *Tesoro della vita humana* (*Treasury of Human Life*) (1570) added numerous endorsements, printed letters from prominent clients and doctors.

Yet at the same time Fioravanti held back certain enticing secrets. He refused to divulge his cure for gout, writing to a physician in 1565: 'I will send you the remedy, but not the secret because I want it [...] Many illustrious men send for this remedy from me and send me many presents, enabling me to study and write.'

As the Englishman Fynes Moryson noted, charlatans commonly sold 'distilled waters and divers oyntments for burning, aches, stitches and the like, but espetially for the itch and scabbs'. Artificial wines were part of the repertoire of smaller-scale operators, such as the 'quintessence of rosemary' retailed in Rome's Piazza Navona by the German distiller, Giovanni Enrico Ugo (1607) and later by Giovan Antonio de Aunno (1611). There are some analogies with Fioravanti's practice, as set out in his *Della fisica* (*On Physic*) (1582), which has a short section on medicinal wines including the above recipe for gout and one for a similar quintessence of 'rosemary wine'.

A HEALTHY LIFE

My rule has always been to get up early and eat in the morning. The first glass of wine I drink in the morning is the best I can get hold of; I have never eaten more than twice a day [...] every evening I go early to bed and never go out at night, like many crazy people, who go around consuming their life [...] In my life, I've never taken any medicine, though it's true that every spring I take *soldanella* [bindweed] which is common here. Each time I take it, it makes me throw up my guts and leaves my stomach so clean that I don't get sick for the entire year. Also, every year, each morning in May, I take three sprigs of rue, three of wormwood and three of rosemary and leave them to infuse in a glass of good wine overnight. Then I drink this in the morning on an empty stomach. I do this for fifteen or twenty mornings, and every year.

* * * * * * * * *
* * * * * * *
* * * *
*

Title page, *Tesoro di secreti naturali* (*Treasury of Natural Secrets*) (Rome, Venice, Milan, Siena, Bologna, Pesaro and Macerata, 2nd edition 1619).

Ferguson Collection, Glasgow University Library, Department of Special Collections: Ag-c.61.

TESORO
DI SECRETI
NATVRALI

Dispensato da me Tomaso da Francolino detto l'Ortolano.

IL VILANO.

In Roma, Bologna, Piacenza, Venetia, & in Verona, Per l'ortolamio Merlo. 1619. Con lic.de' Super.

Historiated Letter N from Book 29, on remedies from animals from Gregorio Piccolomini's manuscript of *Historia naturalis* by Pliny the Elder, Italy, 1460s. This letter illustrates one of Pliny's many chapters that discuss medical remedies. The recipes include a myriad of ingredients, with many derived from animals. A 1st-century Roman writer, Pliny combined direct observation with references to earlier classical sources, such as Aristotle. This encyclopaedic and influential work was a respected source of scientific knowledge in the 15th century, and the printing of an Italian translation in 1478 led to its wide dissemination.

V&A: MSL/1896/1504

A further example of circularity between high and low culture is a short anti-plague recipe touted in a pamphlet by a charlatan, who went by the stage-name of '*L'Ortolano*' ('The Market Gardener', see illustration). His remedy comprises 'three sprigs of rue, a walnut, a dried fig, a garlic clove, eaten on a empty stomach'. This recipe, present in many books of secrets, actually derives from Pliny, and was the famous antidote (theriac) of King Mithridates: 'two dried walnuts, two figs and twenty leaves of rue pounded together with a pinch of salt'.

According to Adam Fox, it was in the form of proverbs that people carried much of their knowledge of medicine and healthy living. Some sixteenth-century English examples still prevalent today include: 'eat an apple before going to bed'; 'make the physician beg his bread'; and 'stuff a cold and starve a fever'. An anonymous Italian pamphlet of secrets, *Il nuovo, vago e dilletevole giardino* (*The New, Lovely and Delightful Garden [of Secrets]*) (Bologna, 1617) synthesises essential 'rules of life' into a short rhyme:

Mangia poco e bevi meno	Eat little and drink less
Alla lussuria pono freno	Curb lust
Dormì in palco, e stà coperto	Sleep on an upper floor and cover up
Lunga cura non ti ponga	Don't subject yourself to long cures
Se vuoi havere tua vita longa	If you want to have a long life

MEDICI ANTI-POISON OIL

TAKE ONE AND A HALF POUNDS OF VINTAGE OIL AND SCORPIONS collected on canicular days [immediately preceding and following the rising of the dog star], purged for two weeks on basil in a cool and dark place. Immerse [the scorpions] in the oil in a glass vessel, the capacity of 1.5 flasks [approximately 3 litres]. Stop with parchment or a bladder so it is airtight. Place in the sun for forty days. Next place in an alembic [of silver or glass] over a vigorous bain-marie for ten hours, and whilst hot, press and extract the oil. Add equal parts of the following drugs to the pressed oil: high-quality rhubarb (1.5 ounces), aloe succotrina (1.5 ounces), spikenard (1.5 ounces), myrrh (1.5 ounces), saffron (1.5 ounces); gentian (6 grams), tormentil (6 grams), Cretan dittany (6 grams), bistort (6 grams); seven-year-old theriac (3 ounces) and Mithridate (3 ounces).

Infuse for two weeks in the sun [...] Strain, press whilst hot, keep in an airtight vessel and use in the following way. Works against all sorts of poisons [both 'live' and 'dead'] ingested by mouth, stings and bites. Anoint the arteries of the head, the fontanel, around the heart and the pulse points of the arms and feet every six hours for both sexes, or more frequently according to need and the particular effects of the poison.

Title page with author portrait from Pier Andrea Mattioli, *Commentaries on Dioscorides' De materia medica* (Venice, 1565).

V&A/NAL: Special Collections 87.A.31

This was not just a remedy; this was a Medici remedy, prepared according to the Grand Duke's own recipe by the Florentine apothecary Stefano Rosselli (see p.91). Francesco I (d.1587) personally conducted experiments into poison antidotes in his laboratories at the Casino (installed in 1587 in the Uffizi) with research and production overseen by expert distillers such as Niccolò Sisti (see p.27). Following the classical example of King Mithridates, it is known that earlier experimenters in both Florence and Rome tried out their poisons and antidotes on condemned criminals.

A similar preoccupation with alchemical medicines is evident in many princely courts of the late sixteenth century, but only Philip II of Spain at the Escorial ever matched the scale of this operation. Antidotes (with attached recipes) were regularly exchanged in the Medici diplomatic and family correspondence. For example, Francesco sent recipes for anti-poison oil and for the Florentine version of the elixir of life in 1561 to Don Pedro de Luna in Sicily, requesting that the Duke not share them with others. But the family went one step further, actually marketing these remedies. In 1600, five hundred copies of this recipe were ordered from the printer Giorgio Marescotti, along with those for ducal 'anti-poison powder', 'spasm oil' and 'nerve oil'. Medici printed recipes evidently circulated widely as transcriptions can be found in sources such as the Bardi family compilation of secrets (see p.43). The same formulas also circulated earlier among Florentine apothecaries, who transcribed them directly from the manuscript records of the ducal laboratories.

The Duke's recipe is a version of the celebrated physician Pier Andrea Mattioli's 'oil of scorpions', as set out in the 1548 edition of his *Commentaries on Dioscorides*. At the vanguard of the efforts to restore and surpass the famous all-purpose cures of the ancients, theriac and mithridate, Mattioli created his own compound, combining the ingredients of both. His more complex formula specifies 100-year-old oil and all the procedures and ingredients specified in the Medici recipe, except that the rhubarb and myrrh are in the form of distilled oils.

A Plague Amulet

MATERIAL FOR MAKING AMULETS OR TALISMANS IN CONJUNCTION with planetary influence: 2 ounces of toads, dried in the heat of the sun and the open air, reduced to a powder with a pestle. Make sure your nostrils are blocked or turn away your head. Eighteen toads yield around 2 ounces of powder. The menstrual blood of young maidens, as much as can be got. White crystalline arsenic; 1.5 ounces of red arsenic or the same amount of orpiment [arsenic sulphide]. 3 drams of root of dittany or the same of tormentil. A dram of unpierced pearls. A dram of coral. One dram each of fragments of eastern sapphire and eastern emerald. Two scruples of eastern saffron. Several grains of musk or ambergris can be added, for their fragrance.

Everything must be ground to a fine powder and mingled. Next, dissolve gum tragacanth in rosewater until it becomes a viscous fluid. Form this and the powders into a paste, and when the Sun and Moon are in Scorpio, or the Moon is very new, shape into round amulets and imprint them with the two seals engraved under that same celestial influence. Alternatively, you can prepare these protective discs in the shape of a heart. Once dry, sew them up in red muslin, and hang them between your shirt and other garments in the region of the heart.

Uses: hang around the neck by a silk ribbon under your shirt in the region of the heart. Preserves not only from the plague but makes the body less vulnerable to venereal or astral diseases. Draws out poison from within, and consumes it from without.

✳ ✳ ✳ ✳ ✳ ✳ ✳ ✳ ✳
✳ ✳ ✳ ✳ ✳ ✳
✳ ✳ ✳
✳

Illustrations from the English translation of *Basilica chymica*, augmented by John Hartman (London, 1670). The plague amulet was inserted into a little iron cylinder engraved on the top with a serpent, on the bottom with a scorpion.

Wellcome Library, London: 19166/C, pp.135, 137

The form of the Inſtrument.

The form of the Inſtrument.

The Swiss medical reformer Paracelsus (1493–1541) regarded the universe as teeming with occult hidden forces. Man, viewed as a microcosm, was at the centre of a complex system of hidden correspondences, linked along lines of sympathy and antipathy; the human body, created by divine alchemy, consisted of mineral and astral components. Disease was not caused by an imbalance of the humours but was seen as an external thing, triggered, for example, by poisonous emanations from the stars. His therapies were revolutionary – chemical remedies in place of regimens, based on the principle of 'like cures like'. Amulet therapy that harnessed astral or sympathetic powers was therefore seen as an effective means of warding off plague.

The secret opposite, known as the *zenexton*, appears in the *Basilica chymica* (*Royal Chemistry*) (1609) by the Paracelsian physician Oswald Croll, based at the Prague court of Rudolf II, the Holy Roman Emperor. This court was a truly European powerhouse of art and science and a magnet for practitioners of the occult arts. A Venetian observer noted that anyone in possession of 'natural and artificial secrets' would 'always find the ears of the Emperor ready': he was a man deeply fascinated by alchemy and natural magic.

The recipe drew on persisting ancient and medieval beliefs that amulets operated by invisible natural forces, on astral magic and the magical properties ascribed to precious stones. Anselm Boëtius de Boodt, Imperial physician at Prague, wrote in 1609 that ruby 'resists poisons and repels the plague'; similarly, Gerolamo Cardano stated that emeralds (used in this recipe) 'annul the effects of poison because of their porosity'.

Vannoccio Biringuccio noted in 1540: 'it is said that it is a remedy against the plague to carry them [realgar, orpiment and arsenic] in a little bag over the heart'. Yet it would be wrong to suggest that this remedy, employing an array of 'deadly and rank poisons', notably arsenic, did not arouse controversy. In England, even Pierre Drouet, a convinced Paracelsian, in *A New Counsell against the Plague* (1578), mentioned the risk of ulcers caused by wearing arsenic lozenges 'folded in a double piece of silk' against the skin. The harmful effects of such 'plague cakes' were vigorously debated in pamphlets by the doctors Francis Herrin and Peter Turner (London, 1603/4).

Detail from Antonio Tempesta, *Gennaio* (January), engraving. Italy (1599). In the foreground, birds are being plucked and roasted on spits in the kitchen by servants and cooks for guests in the *sala* (the largest room in the house) beyond. Other game is hung above the scullery.

V&A: 29283A

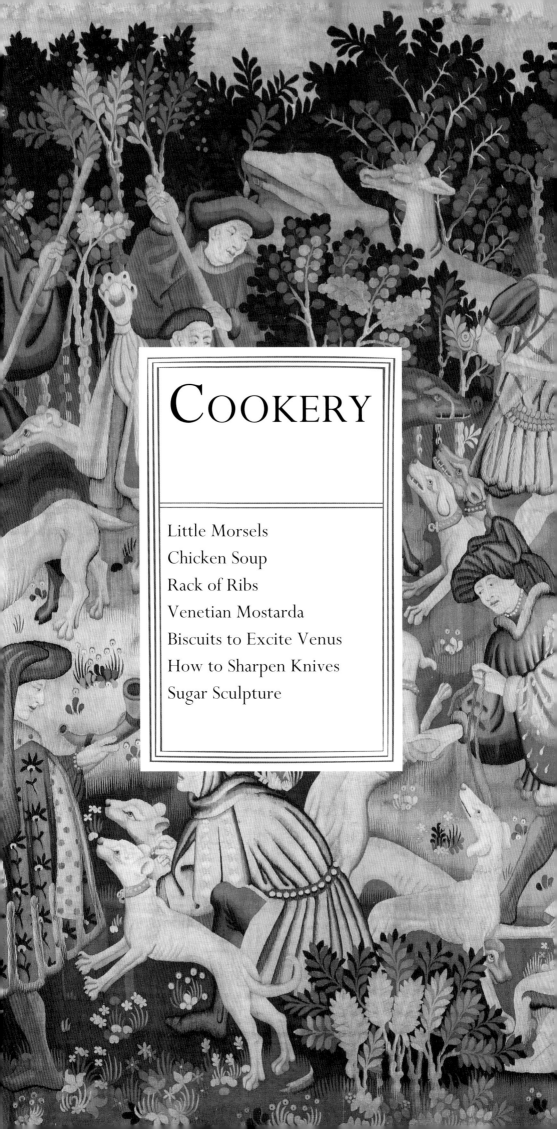

COOKERY

LITTLE MORSELS

To make *mostaccioli* as they use in Naples, a delicacy for every great Prince, which comfort the stomach and make a sweet breath

TAKE 3 POUNDS OF FINE SUGAR, 6 POUNDS OF HIGH-GRADE FLOUR, 3 ounces of cinnamon, and half an ounce each of nutmeg, ginger and pepper. But take slightly more pepper than the other spices. [Also take] 3 pounds of raw white honey – do not clarify it.

First, make a circle with the flour, and put the sugar in the middle, and add a pound of rosewater. Work well with your hands until you can no longer feel the sugar. Next add the spices, then the honey. Mix well all this together with your hands.

Next, mix this again with the flour, keeping back enough flour to dust the [baking] tile. And once it is well mixed to a paste, cut the morsels with your hands, making each of them 3 ounces in weight. Then shape them into the form of a fish, with your cutter. Heat your oven, and lay them on little earthenware or copper tiles, on a thick bed of flour. And bake them with the mouth of the oven open, always keeping a fire at one of the sides of the oven. Touch them often to see if they are cooked, lift easily and hold together in your fingers

[…] Take them out and gild them.

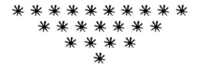

From the sample menus in Bartolomeo Scappi's culinary treatise (the source of the illustration) we know that these biscuits were eaten at the start not the end of a meal. They were served from the *credenza* (sideboard) as part of a first course of cold foods consisting of marzipan, biscuits, *capi di latte* (a sort of cream), fruits and 'salads' consisting of sliced meats, fish and shellfish of all kinds.

This recipe, as Elizabeth David noted, was first printed in the most famous book of secrets of the Renaissance, *Secreti del reverendo donno Alessio Piemontese* (*The Secrets of Don Alessio Piemontese*) (Venice, 1555). An instant bestseller, it rapidly appeared in Latin, French and Dutch editions. It was through this source, translated from the French by William Warde as *The Secretes of the Reuerende Maister Alexis of Piemount,* that Italian confectionary recipes reached England in 1558.

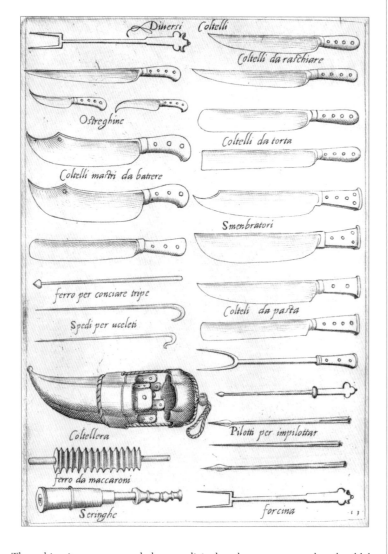

These biscuits were regarded as medicinal and were prepared and sold by apothecaries. However, there is considerable variation amongst surviving recipes for *morseletti* (or *mostaccioli alla napoletana*) from these traders. The Florentine apothecary Stefano Rosselli supplies a recipe 'of his own invention' in his manuscript of secrets intended for his sons, dated 1593. In this, the main ingredients are high-grade flour, pounded sugar, ground almonds, and egg yolks. The spices included are cinnamon, musk and ambergris. A firm paste can be made by adding rosewater. The biscuits are baked in tin moulds, and then gilded. In the manuscript secrets of another Florentine *speziale* (apothecary) Pietro Paolo di Carlo Beccuti Scala, the paste is made from finely pounded sugar, cinnamon and ten egg yolks, to which marzipan paste, two egg whites and cloves are added. The biscuits were then cut into the typical rhomboid shapes associated with *mostaccioli*. Dusted with sugar and rosewater, they were baked at a low heat.

The extent of Arabic influence on such medicinal foodstuffs has yet to be fully traced but the famous Baghdad cookbook of 1226 contains a similar recipe for biscuits made from sugar, honey, musk, rosewater and starch pounded into a paste and pressed into wooden moulds shaped liked loaves and fishes.

CHICKEN SOUP

To make a tasty broth of capons

SOME CONSIDER THIS BROTH TO BE MARVELLOUS FOR CONVALESCENTS, but I have made it to order for physicians many times. Take a capon chopped in pieces as above [as small as possible, rinsing once to remove any blood, cover with water and boil], simmer gently in a pan until you have removed all the scum that rises to the surface. With an earthenware lid over the pan, leave to simmer for one hour with a thin slice of prosciutto […] which adds taste to the broth and satisfies the listless. Remove the prosciutto […] and add an eighth of an ounce of cinnamon. Let it reduce by more than half its original volume, strain through a sieve and make a minestra from this broth, as it is more suitable for minestre and little fine broths than to give as a drink.

* * * * * * * * *
* * * * * * *
* * * *
*

Maiolica *scodella*, made in Northern Italy (Castel Durante), probably painted by Nicola da Urbino, *c*.1533–8. This bowl is decorated with typical childbirth scenes and would have held nourishing soup for the new mother. The lid shows both the birth and an astrologer divining the child's future. A second scene at the bottom of the bowl, which depicts the newborn baby, would have been revealed when the bowl was emptied.

V&A: C.2258&A–1910

COOKERY

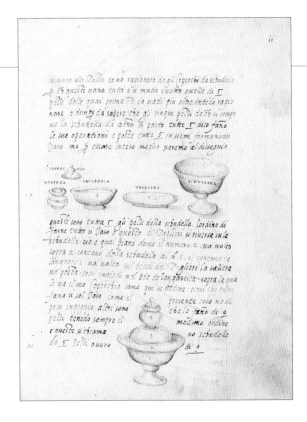

Capons are 'more nutritious than all other foods […] generate perfect blood and balance all the humours', according to Castor Durante, *Il Tesoro della sanità* (*The Treasury of Health*) (1585). The recipe above comes from the final part of Bartolomeo Scappi's famous cookbook (see p.87), which deals with foods for 'convalescents'. This broth was generally considered by physicians like Ulisse Aldrovandi to be the ideal food to 'rally the sinking strength of their patients', above all for the elderly, the feverish and women in pregnancy and childbirth. So when the wife of Miho Bunic, a Dubrovnik nobleman, aged 36, contracted fever after having twins (one of which died instantly after birth), her expert physician, Amatus Lusitanus, prescribed capon broth and other invigorating foods (porridge and watermelon seeds). Leonardo Fioravanti (see p.73) in his *Compendio dei secreti naturali* (*Compendium of Natural Secrets*) (Venice, 1564) supplied a recipe for this broth, 'called *brodo consumato* in Rome, *sorcicco* in Naples and *consumato* in Venice', along with others for highly nutritious 'little fine broths' (with eggs, parsley or other herbs) for the sick. He called for sugar to be added, which Scappi similarly included in his first and longer recipe for *brodo consumato* (intended as a drink). Walther Hermann Ryff, the prolific author of books of secrets for 'the common man', also provided a recipe for chicken soup in his *Kochbüch für die Krancken* (*Cookbook for the Sick*) (Frankfurt, 1545), for Germany's leading publisher, Christian Egenolff.

Special maiolica wares for childbirth (including maiolica and wooden bowls for these broths) were commonly given as gifts in Renaissance Italy. Illustrated here from the Piccolpasso manuscript (see p.23) is one example, a five-piece stacking set, comprising a salt cellar, bowl, trencher, bowl on a high foot and its lid, 'a thing of no small ingenuity'. These sets (and simpler ones of just a bowl plus lid) were referred to as '*scodella da impagliata*' (childbirth bowls).

Other reviving superfoods given to women before and after birth included *zabaglione*, with recipes in both Scappi and *La Commare* (*The Midwife*) (Venice, 1596) by the Roman physician Scipione Mercurio. In England, new mothers were given posset – warm milk curdled with ale, spiced and often thickened with eggs – and the V&A has several specially designed two-handled posset pots (in the British Galleries). In Italy, following childbirth, friends and relatives brought refreshments on specially painted wooden trays (*deschi da parto*), generally special treats purchased from apothecaries, such as comfits – sugar-coated aniseed or coriander seeds.

RACK OF RIBS

IF THE PIG IS YOUNG, THE RACK CAN BE ROASTED ON THE SPIT (with or without the skin), with chopped onions in the drip pan, which cook in the fat that falls from it […] And put some slivers of rosemary inside the rack of ribs. Dust with salt and ground coriander seed before placing on the spit. The rack can also be left to marinate for a day in vinegar, cooked grape must, garlic cloves and ground coriander seeds. Then spit-roast in the aforesaid manner; serve hot with a sauce made from the same marinade above. If you want to make Venetian style cutlets from the rack, cut it rib from rib, and pound the said cutlets with the back of a knife. Sprinkle with salt, coarsely ground pepper and ground coriander seed; and when they have been [pressed] one on top of another for an hour, cook them on the grill over a slow fire, turning often.

Once cooked, serve them with a sauce made from bitter oranges or other sauces above.

Boar and Bear Hunt tapestry (detail). Southern Netherlands, *c.*1425–30. Although the background depicts lush foliage, wild boar were usually hunted during the winter when their flesh was flavoured by a diet of acorns, nuts and truffles. Hunting was an important, ritualized, leisure activity for the European elite, and as well as providing for the table, presented a chance to prove bravery and skill in peacetime.

V&A: T.204–1957

Title page of Giulio Cesare Croce, *L'Eccellenza, et trionfo del porco* (Ferrara, 1594).

By permission of the British Library, London: 976.e.31.(1.)

The aroma of the roast suckling pig thrown to the crowd in Bologna's main square on the Feast of St Bartholomew was so pleasing that it could wake the dead, recounted the Bolognese street poet Giulio Cesare Croce in his pamphlet, *L'eccellenza, et trionfo del porco* (*The Excellence and Triumph of the Pig*) (1594). A trade secret of the silk industry, so he claimed, was to perfume the rooms in which silkworms were bred with the 'great fragrance' of a grilled pork chop. The smell enlivened the worms, encouraged them to adhere to the twigs where they spun their cocoons, and doubled their productivity.

This mouthwatering recipe for roast pork comes from the magisterial *Opera* of Bartolomeo Scappi, based on thirty years' experience of cooking at the highest level. Book Four is filled with sample menus cooked for cardinals and the papal court, and from these we learn that this dish was served hot as part of the first or second service from the kitchen. On 8 December, rack of ribs was matched with *mostarda* in a lunch that began with 'Pisan biscuits in malmsey' served in wine glasses (see p.21) and *mostaccioli* (see p.83). On 8 January, we find it alongside pork tenderloin in a bitter orange sauce, tempered by Scappi with sugar: recipes for both these dishes follow each other in Book Two. Scappi records it again on 16 February, but with a new combination of flavours in the sauce: bitter oranges, olives and sugar.

Scappi's directions show evident similarities with his recipe for the equivalent cut of roast beef: a marinade of salt, ground fennel or coriander seed, coarsely ground pepper and a little garlic; roast the meat with rosemary on a spit (though baste with lard), serve hot with onions. Here though he offers a sauce made from his signature spice mixture, vinegar and cooked grape must. Scappi also uses a seasoning of 'salt, ground coriander seed and coarsely ground pepper' for pork tenderloin. Domenico Romoli has a recipe for the same in his cookbook (Venice, 1560) that also calls for seasoning made from ground coriander and fennel seed, salt and pepper. He recommends a marinade of oregano, ground coriander seed, crushed garlic and pepper, again similar to Scappi.

The *Opera* also refers to rack of ribs seemingly cooked in exactly the same way as the recipe above, this time for *rufalotto* (young wild boar), also matched with *mostarda*. Writers such as Baldassare Pisanelli show a slight preference for boar over domesticated pig since exercise was thought to offset pork's excessive humidity.

Venetian Mostarda

Venetian *mostarda*, more than any other sort in the world, is very healthy for the body, agreeable to the stomach and pleasing to the taste [...] It is made as follows. In October, take quinces, clean them [skin and core], cut into quarters, removing all the pips. Put into a cauldron filled with [good] well water and boil down until all the water evaporates [...] Then add enough *melazzo* [coarse sugar] to cover them completely and boil again, until all the humidity has disappeared. Stir constantly with a wooden stick whilst boiling. Once cooked, remove from the fire and put into suitable preserving jars. This is known as *conserva di mostarda*. When you want to make *mostarda*, take mustard seeds and grind them to a fine powder. Combine with coarse sugar, and add cinnamon, cloves and nutmeg to taste; incorporate the *conserva*. Some also add finely grated orange peel [probably candied peel].

✳✳✳✳✳✳✳✳✳
✳✳✳✳✳✳✳
✳✳✳✳
✳

Maiolica *mostarda* jar. Italian, probably Venetian, 1556. The tin-glazed decoration on this apothecary's drug jar includes a cartouche containing the Latin label 'Mostarda F' (fine *mostarda*). The surrounding jumble of instruments and implements includes a mortar of the sort that may have been used to grind the mustard seeds.

V&A: 2587–1856

ma in quanto al modo di farlo è quasi tutto uno, & si fa così, cioè. Piglia farina, e se gli fa il suo leuato, come si fa per fare il pane, e poi s'impasta con acqua, e mele, tanto d'uno quanto dell'altro, & ui si mette pe[r] zafarano, comino, garofali, zucche condite, scorze di naranze condite, di tutte le dette cose quella quantità, che pare allo Speciale, che si conuenga in detto pane, & impastato che farà, farà il pane, et lasciarlo leuare, & dipoi farlo cuocere nel forno, auertendo che'l forno non sia troppo caldo quando ni si pone il detto pane, & quest'è molto salutifero allo stomaco, rispetto alle spetie, che u'entrano.

Del modo di fare la mostarda che si fa in Venetia. Cap. 40.

LA mostarda che si fa in Venetia è molto salutifera al corpo, grata allo stomaco, e piaceuole al gusto più che tutte l'altre sorti di mostarde, che s'usano in diuersi luochi del mondo, et la detta mostarda si fa in modo tale, cioè. Nel mese d'Ottobre, piglianosi cotogne, et mondansi, et tagliansi in pezzi 4. e gli si cauano le semenze, e s'hanno dentro, nette che sono si mettono a bollire dentro una caldara con acqua di pozzo, e si fanno bollire tanto, che tutta l'acqua sia consumata, & le cotogne restino asciutte, & poi ui s'aggiunge tanto melazzo di zuccaro, che siano tutte coperte, & si fanno bollire tanto, che tutta la humidità dell'acqua sia estinta, & mentre che bollono col

col detto melazzo, sempre tenerle rimenate con un bastone, & come la sopradetta materia è cotta leuar la dal fuoco, & riporla in uasi che siano a conseruarla, & questa si chiama conserua da mostarda, & quando uogliono fare la mostarda, tolgono sciapa, e la macinano sottile, et la incorporano con un nuouo melazzo, & ui pongono canella, garofali, noce moscate quella quantità, che pare all'artefice, & dipoi pigliano della detta conserua, & incorporano tutto insieme, & alcuni u'aggiungono naranzata sottilmente macinata, & questa è la mostarda cordialissima, & buona, che si fa a Venetia, laquale, come ho detto, ella è più perfetta di quante mostarde che si possono fare, come da gli ingredienti si può vedere: perciòche tutti sono cordialissimi, & di molta virtù.

Del modo di fare la mostarda, che s'usa in Lombardia. Cap. 41.

SI usa un'altra sorte di mostarda nelle parti di Lombardia, laquale è questa, cioè. Pigliansi dell'uve passe, & fichi secchi, & si pongono a bollire dentro l'acqua di mele, sin che son benissimo cotti, & poi si macinano con una macina da macinare mostarda, laqual è fatta a posta per tale essercitio, & macinate che sono, si macina senapa con coriandoli, et anisi. Lequal cose si mettono in detta mostarda, & si distemperano con la detta acqua di mele, & questa è la

Recipe for Venetian *mostarda* from Leonardo Fioravanti, *Compendio dei secreti rationali* (Venice, 1564), Bk 5, ch.40.

By permission of the British Library: C.108.s.10

Travelling through Italy, with several lengthy detours to spas to alleviate the pain of his kidney stones, Montaigne sampled local food wherever he went. In October 1581, he was at Fornovo in the Apennines, where he was 'served with *mostarda* – very good – of different kinds', including one made with quinces. The next evening he reached Borgo San Donino, where 'they put on the table *mostarda* made with apples and oranges, cut into slices, like half-cooked quince marmalade (*cotognata*)'. *Mostarda*, a fruit preserve given added bite with ground mustard seeds – classified as a sauce by the professional cook Bartolomeo Scappi (see previous recipe) – was frequently served with boiled meats and pork.

Italian books of secrets contain relatively few recipes for foods. When they do, nearly all of them are for foods sold ready-made by apothecaries and viewed as highly medicinal. *Mostarda* falls firmly into this category (alongside similar quince pastes such as *cotognata*). This is why the recipe opposite was included in the *Compendium of Rational Secrets* (Venice, 1564) by Leonardo Fioravanti (see p.73).

Fioravanti also supplies a recipe for a different sort of *mostarda* from Lombardy, consisting of dried figs and raisins boiled in honey syrup, with the addition of mustard seeds ground together with coriander and aniseed. Scappi provides another for a 'sweet *mostarda*' made from grape must, quinces cooked in wine and sugar, mustard seed, candied lemon peel, candied nutmeg, candied (bitter) orange peel, seasoned with sugar, salt and spices (cinnamon and cloves).

According to the papal physician Castor Durante, *mostarda* wondrously stimulated the appetite, expelled phlegm from the head and corrected liver problems. However, *mostarda* could sometimes penetrate 'disagreeably into the nose and brain' as its vapours were believed to rise (literally 'steam') to the head. Its main ingredients were thought to be especially good for the stomach and digestion. Quinces 'recreate the heart' and 'strengthen and close the mouth of the stomach', wrote Henry Buttes in his *Dyets Dry Dinner* (London, 1599). Eating plenty could even increase the chances of giving birth to sons of marked intellect and energy. Mustard, a good sauce for 'sundry meats and fish', purged the brain and was recommended for the 'old, cold and rheumatic'. Dijon mustard, already famous, also came in dry form and was sold by the city's apothecaries in the fifteenth and sixteenth centuries.

In Renaissance Spain, a condiment called *mostaza* (made from mustard-seeds, honey, vinegar and bread) was recommended by Francisco Núñez de Oria to correct 'gross meats that are difficult to digest, like beef, because it cuts and diminishes their fattiness'.

The maiolica drug jar pictured opposite is one of several in V&A collections labelled as a container for *mostarda*.

BISCUITS TO EXCITE VENUS

Morsels to excite Venus. Proven many times and which increase sperm. They do not cause any harm.

TAKE 3 DRAMS EACH OF WALNUTS, PINE-KERNELS AND PISTACHIO nuts; 3 drams each of powdered seeds of rocket, onion and knotgrass [also referred to as swine-grass or bloodwort]; half a dram each of cloves, cinnamon and ginger; 1.5 ounces of skinned skinks [saltwater lizards], four should suffice – remove the heads and feet and grind to a fine powder; 1 ounce of Indian nut [coconut]; 1 dram each of long pepper, galangal, seeds of wild asparagus, chickpeas (the red variety); 3 ounces of diasatirion; a dram of ambergris; half a dram of musk; 12 ounces of sugar dissolved in rosewater. Make *morseletti* in the normal way.

Statuette of Venus Callipygos, probably by Anthony Susini. Bronze, Italy (Florence), *c.*1600. This excellent cast of a draped Venus, turning to admire her own buttocks, is freely based on an antique marble statue that had recently been excavated in Rome, at the site of the Emperor Nero's Golden House.

V&A: A.141–1910

Giovanni Balducci (known as Cosci), *Mars and Venus surprised by Vulcan*. Ink pen and wash on blue paper, heightened with white, Italy, 1550–1600. Venus, the goddess of love and wife of Vulcan, is about to be discovered entwined with Mars in her marital bed. Variations on this classical scene were popular as an erotic subject in 16th-century Italian art, derived from both Homer's *Odyssey* and Ovid's *Metamorphoses*.

V&A: D.123–1888

These biscuits packed a punch. Pistachio nuts were 'wondrous for stimulating sexual desire', even if they were fattening, according to Baldassare Pisanelli in his *Trattato della natura de' cibi e del bere* (*Treatise on the Nature of Foods and Drink*) (Rome, 1583). Pine-nuts similarly 'greatly increased sperm'. The Roman writers Pliny and Dioscorides both identified rocket as a powerful aphrodisiac. They agreed too about skink: Pliny recommended this lizard's 'snout and feet taken in white wine' combined with satyrion and rocket seed. Caterina Sforza claimed an ounce was enough to 'keep you always hard. You can do it as much as you like and the woman can do her business.' Similarly, chickpeas excited Venus and coconuts increased sperm, according to Castor Durante's *Treasury of Health* (see p.85).

The killer ingredient though was *diasatirion*, an approved compound sold by apothecaries, frequently attributed to the great Arab physician Yuhanna ibn Masawaih (known in the West as Mesue, d.857). Known as 'wolf's testicles', it was based on the bulbous roots of an orchid, satyrion. In its most common form, *diasatirion* comprised chickpeas, skinks, the brain of sparrows (infamous for provoking lust), ginger and cinnamon. A variant formula in the standard pharmaceutical manual (based on Mesue) the *Luminare maius* also included pistachio nuts, pine-nuts, musk, sea holly, aniseed, rocket seeds and parsnip.

These biscuits were clearly intended for men – especially as the Florentine apothecary Stefano Rosselli (from whom the recipe opposite is taken) also stocked a rub, which customers were to use to get an erection, after eating the biscuits. He evidently did a brisk trade, as he provided another recipe for 'similar morsels' sold 'for a long time' with 'great effects', and 'sent many times to Rome'. Caterina Sforza, however, in her early fifteenth-century recipe collection, noted down a number of substances that worked equally well for both sexes: 'Linseed mixed with pepper, drunk in wine ignites lust'; 'the powdered seeds of nettles, mixed with pepper and honey, drunk in wine, excites all'. However, as Shakespeare famously noted of drink (*Macbeth* 2.3), 'It provokes the desire, but it takes away the performance. Therefore much drink may be said to be an equivocator with lechery: it makes him and it mars him; it sets him on and it takes him off.'

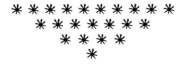

How to Sharpen Knives

Since everyone, whatever his profession, is obliged to keep his books, weapons, tools and other such things in order, according to his profession, so every carver is obliged to keep his knives in working order [...] Wishing to clean and sharpen them, follow the instructions below. Take a piece of willow, two hands long and two fingers wide, and plane it all over. Clamp onto a bench top (or wherever you please) so it will not move around. Sprinkle well-dried and finely ground grit such as falls from the grinder's whetstone or other similar 'sand' [abrasive] over the willow. Next, grip your knife by the handle and draw it lightly across the willow – this demands much nimbleness and skill – until you see both sides of the blade and handle are clean. To sharpen, sprinkle the filings on the said willow again. Grasp the knife firmly by the handle, and with great dexterity draw both sides of the blade across the willow in the direction of the tip. When the knife is warm to the touch [... sharpen the edges] taking care to hone both sides evenly and consistently; to test its sharpness, draw the knife over your thumbnail, if it nicks the nail, it is sharp enough.

Carving set. Steel, with jasper handles and silver gilt mounts, Germany, 1450–1500. Carving was such an important and public activity at banquets that these decorated sets were made of precious materials, befitting the status of the host. As described in *Il Trinciante*, the traditional German method of carving and presenting required rounded knives and long handled forks. The meat was carved on a dish rather than in mid-air.

V&A: 1165:1–5–1864

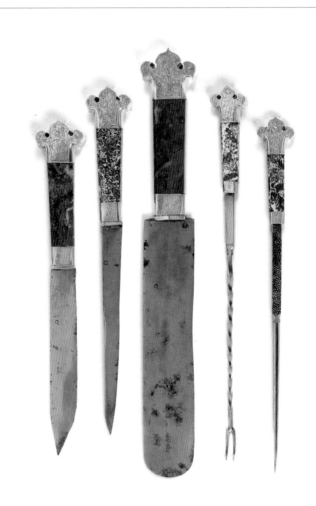

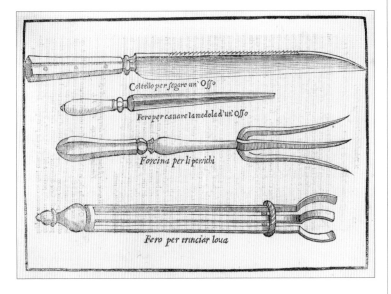

Coltello per segare un' Osso.

Fero per cauare la medola d'un' Osso.

Forcina per li perseichi.

Fero per trinciar loua.

Woodcut illustration of implements from Vincenzo Cervio, *Il Trinciante* (*The Carver*), (Venice, 1581). 1593 edition; printed by Gabbia for G. Buchioni.

V&A/NAL: 87.C.82

Meat-carving was raised to the level of an art form in Renaissance Italy. In breathtaking displays of control and grace, the most skilled professionals at the cardinals' courts at Rome carved in mid-air, keeping even massive joints aloft on a fork high over the plate. An exhaustive description of the secrets of this 'profession' appeared in *Il Trinciante* (*The Carver*) (Venice, 1581), published after the death of the master-carver Vincenzo Cervio, who had served both Duke Guidobaldo II of Urbino and Cardinal Alessandro Farnese (1520–89). The manual had been 'expanded and perfected' by his successor, cavalier Fusoritto da Narni, and was addressed to an apprentice. 'Those wishing to learn to carve must first know how forks and knives are made and tempered, how they are cleaned and sharpened, how they should be held, how to use them and the posture to adopt when using them.' But the author's first concern was to present this trade as a 'noble profession', as the Roman courts were by then in such dire straits that carvers were being paid 15 or 20 *giuli* a month, a salary fit for a 'stable hand'. So different from Cervio's day, when carvers had received 'attire', 'servants', 'horses' and handsome pensions.

The expertise of the master-carver in handling and maintaining knives was one of the qualities which marked him as a cut above the lowly 'butcher' or 'barber'; his tools were always spotless and razor-sharp. The text is equally perfectionist about the exact types of knives and matching forks required for specific meats – chapters clearly inspired by the carving treatise dedicated to Alfonso d'Este, Duke of Ferrara by the noble Giovan Francesco Colle, *Refugio de povero gentilhuomo* (1520). Cesare Evitascandolo's dialogue on the carver (1609), supposedly composed during the terrible plague of 1576 in Venice, provides further advice on storing knives in bran or lime and preventing rust by smearing them with bone marrow and a little sugar. According to Ottaviano Rabasco (1609), many carvers in Rome indeed demonstrated the secrets of 'this respected profession' to apprentices: after observing the master in action, schooling included practising carving on hardened bread and white cabbages before graduating onto animals.

SUGAR SCULPTURE

TO MAKE SUGAR PASTE, WITH WHICH YOU CAN MOULD ALL MANNER of fruits and other fine things that please you […] such as plates, bowls, dishes, glasses, cups and other similar things to furnish a table. At the end of the meal they can be eaten; a thing of great pleasure and wonder. Take as much gum tragacanth as you like. Steep in rosewater until it softens. For every 4 ounces of sugar, take one bean's worth of the gum and a little lemon juice [a walnut shell full] and egg white. First pound the gum in a mortar of white marble or bronze until it becomes watery. Next, add the lemon juice and the yolk, incorporating well together. Then take 4 ounces of fine white powdered sugar. Cast it into the mortar little by little until it turns into a paste. Remove from the mortar. Dust with powdered sugar so it becomes a soft paste [as you would flour dough] that you can shape and mould as you wish […] Roll out into thin and thick sheets as you see fit.

✳ ✳ ✳ ✳ ✳ ✳ ✳ ✳ ✳
✳ ✳ ✳ ✳ ✳ ✳
✳ ✳ ✳ ✳
✳

Probably by Antonio Susini, after Giambologna, statuette of Morgante blowing a trumpet. Bronze, Italy (Florence), c.1580–90. As the Medici court jester, the dwarf Baccio di Bartolo ('Il Morgante') was a celebrated 16th-century figure. He was famed for allegedly wrestling a monkey for the amusement of Grand Duke Cosimo I, of whom he was a particular favourite. A sugar paste sculpture of Morgante on a barrel formed part of the table decorations at a banquet celebrating Prince Cosimo's marriage in 1608, probably derived from another bronze statuette attributed to Giambologna.

V&A: 65–1864

Recipe for sugar paste ('far una pasta di zucchero') from Part 1, Bk 3, of *Secreti del reverendo donno Alessio Piemontese*, 2nd edition (Venice, 1557).

By permission of the British Library, London: 42.f.19, pp.100–1

Brussels, 18 November 1565. An incredible sugar collation, a gift from the city of Antwerp, was served at the marriage festivities of Alessandro Farnese, Duke of Parma and Piacenza, and Maria of Portugal, cousin of Philip II of Spain. A commemorative booklet by the Bolognese Francesco de Marchi records that all the plates, bowls, knives, forks, glasses, and candlesticks, and even the bread were sculpted in sugar. Still more astounding was a panorama of Brussels made from sugar, so detailed that even the dice games and card tables inside palaces could be made out. An equally lavish display was organised in Venice in 1574 to honour Henry III of France on his return from Warsaw as King of Poland. At the Arsenal (state-run dockyards), the sugar show was so convincing that the King reached for a napkin, only for it to crumble in his grasp. At the ball at the Ducal Palace, Henry was treated to over 300 sugar statues of 'animals, monsters, dwarves and griffons', created by the apothecary Niccolò della Pigna. The showpiece was 14 figures (including one of a queen astride two tigers, emblazoned with the arms of France and Poland) based on designs by the sculptors Jacopo Sansovino and Danese Cattaneo.

Trade secrets detailing how to cast fruits and model sugar paste in wooden and bronze moulds (into caskets, glasses, cups, vases, shoes and fans), as produced for the Medici wedding of 1589, were noted down for his sons by the apothecary Stefano Rosselli (see p.83). One formula was supplied by another leading *speziale* (apothecary), Coriolano Osio Veronese, who cast numerous sugar animals in moulds from bronzes and later restored several created with the Giambologna workshop (see illustration opposite).

This recipe was the first in English for sugar paste (from the 1558 translation of *Secreti del reverendo donno Alessio Piemontese*, shown above). The original Italian version is reproduced above. Court fashions could now be recreated at home. By 1602, Hugh Plat's *Delightes for Ladies* presented sugar sculpture as an essential skill for elite housewives to adorn their tables, part of the domestic 'arte of preserving, conserving and candying'. It instructed how to cast figures such as rabbits and pigeons either from life or in carved moulds – 'rare' and 'strange' devices and forms of 'sweetest grace'. Plat (see p.55) practised the art of moulding himself professionally (in plaster, wax and glue), exploiting a growing demand for all kinds of moulded figures for domestic interiors, and he devoted an entire section of his *Jewell House of Art and Nature* (1594) to these techniques.

Der Papyrer.

Ich brauch Hadern zu meiner Mül
Dran treibt mirs Rad deß waſſers viel/
Daß mir die zſchnitn Hadern nelt/
Das zeug wirt in waſſer einquelt/
Drauß mach ich Pogn/auff dē filtz bring/
Durch preß das waſſer darauß zwing.
Denn henck ichs auff/laß drucken wern/
Schneweiß vnd glatt/ ſo hat mans gern.
F ij   Der

J ost Amman, The Papermaker, woodcut. From the *Eygentliche Beschreibung aller Stände auff Erden … (Exact Description of all Ranks on Earth … of all Crafts and Trades etc.)* (Frankfurt, 1568). This *Book of Trades* with verses by Hans Sachs, the shoemaker poet from Nuremberg, included illustrations by Amman of 114 trades. The accompanying verse reads 'Rags are brought unto my mill / Where much water turns the wheel / They are cut, and shorn, and shredded / To the pulp, the water is added; / Then the sheets between felts I lay / Whilst I wring them in my press. / Lastly, I hang them up to dry / Snow-white in glossy loveliness'.

V&A/NAL: Special Collections, 86.D.46

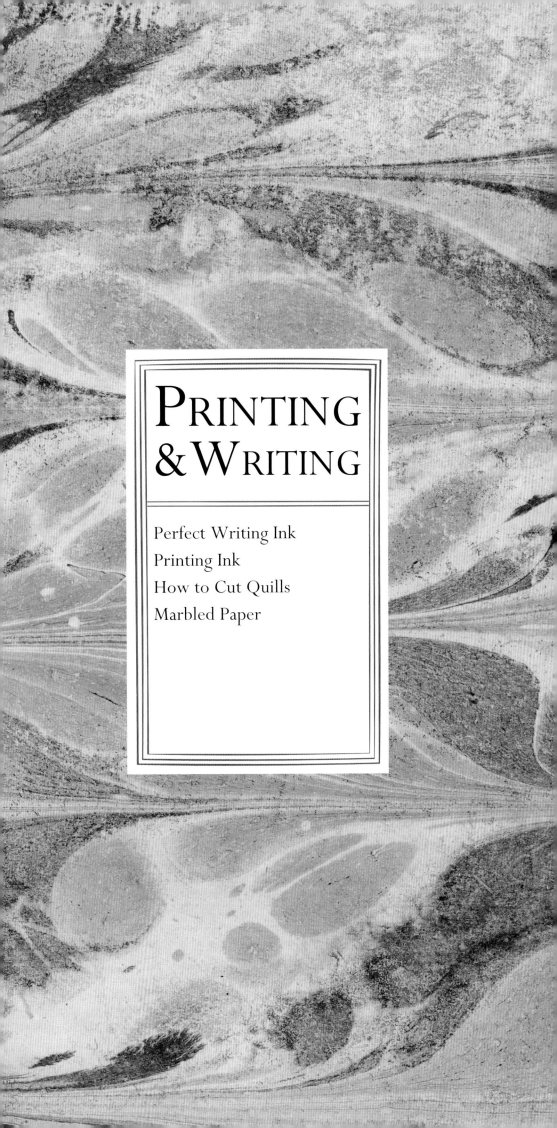

PRINTING & WRITING

PERFECT WRITING INK

TAKE AN OUNCE OF GALLNUTS [OAK-GALLS] CRUSHED INTO LITTLE
pieces. Then put into a linen cloth. Tie it up, but not too tightly.
Leave to soak for at least six days in 12 ounces of rainwater.
Next, boil until it reduces down to 8 ounces. Strain and add
a quarter ounce of German vitriol, ground to a fine powder
and half an ounce of gum arabic, steeped in vinegar [...]
And you will make a wondrously good ink.

✳ ✳ ✳ ✳ ✳ ✳ ✳ ✳ ✳
✳ ✳ ✳ ✳ ✳ ✳ ✳
✳ ✳ ✳ ✳
✳

Inkstand in two parts
depicting the figure of
Hope. Cast bronze, Italy
(Venice), 1550–1600.
Three lions support each
corner of the triangular
container, which would
probably have been
fitted with a lead lining
to hold the ink. Such
pieces combined a
practical function with
the humanist scholar's
practice of collecting
and displaying small
bronzes in the study.

V&A: 567&A–1865

consumi la terza parte, & puoi leuato dal fuoco, meterea-
ui dentro Gomma rabica ben trita: tanto che basti facendo-
ne la proua in su la piana della mano, & fatto questo po
nilo al Sole per dui giorni, & per dui altri giorni lo farai
star scoperto al' ombra in luoco doue non d a la serenata;
ne mancho acqua, puoi quando sera alquanto riposato colalo
con vna pezzetta di tela di lino bianha, & serbalo in vno
vaso de vetro & sara perfetto.

Recetta da fare inchiostro fino.
Togli vna oncia di Galleto pisto in pezzetti, & puoi lo met
terai in vna pezza di tela, & ligaralla, non troppo stret-
ta & metteralla a mollo in. xij. oncie d'acqua, che sia proua
na, & lassalo stare almen sei giorni, & fatto questo falla
bollire tanto che torni otto oncie bello e colato & puoi met
terai dentro vn quarto de vetriolo Tolefo molto ben spol
uerizato, & meza oncia di Gomma che sis stata a molle
in aceto & che l'aceto non sia piu del bisogno & tu farai
vno inchiostro mirabilmente buono.

Alli Lettori gratissimi.
I puoi che noi siamo con la diuina
prouidentia arriuato al porto della
promissione, che gia ne 'l nostro,
general probemio fidelme te prome
tessimo con summa arte, & dili-
gentia tutte le particolare; & ge-
nerale sorte de lettere, e con quelle
vie, modi, & secreti, che siano stati per hora possibile

By 1522, Ugo da Carpi was a renowned and highly skilled engraver. Six years earlier he had secured exclusive rights from the Venetian Senate for a 'new way of printing in light and shade' – the chiaroscuro woodcut. He obtained the privilege for importing a new and useful technique into the state, not for being its original inventor. Although 'something new and never done before' in Italy, the chiaroscuro print was developed in Germany by artists such as Burgkmair and Cranach. Now based in Rome, Ugo had won fame for making such prints after drawings (or prints from them) from Raphael's workshop. He had teamed up with a professional scribe, Ludovico degli Arrighi (called Vicentino), to produce a handwriting manual, planned for publication that year, designed to teach the elegant and rapid cursive script used in the papal chancery. This work is now recognized as the most influential writing-book on italic ever written. Yet when the first edition appeared (1523/4), Arrighi had Ugo's name deliberately obliterated from its final page.

In retaliation, Ugo not only secured a papal privilege to issue his own edition, he also compiled and published his own anthology, the *Thesauro de scrittori* (*Writers' Treasury*) (Rome, 1525). The ink formula above comes from this work, the only writing-book by a sixteenth-century artist.

Hundreds of recipes for writing ink survive from the Renaissance. The great majority are for iron-gall inks, common from the twelfth century. The basic formula was common knowledge, so as Leonardo Fioravanti noted, whilst these recipes differ slightly in their making, 'all include galls and vitriol'. Oak-galls contain gallotannic and gallic acids, released in the recipes by soaking in water or wine and often (as above) by boiling over a slow fire. In reaction with iron II sulphate, these acids produce a pigment, which blackens on exposure to air. Italian recipes frequently call for Roman vitriol (grass-green in colour) or copperas. German vitriol (imported into Venice and yellowish green in colour) is less common. The viscosity and flow of this ink was controlled with gum arabic, which kept the pigment in suspension and added brilliance, binding the ink at the paper surface and reducing the speed at which it bit into the fibres. Variations produced inks that were stiffer or more fluid, performed better in summer or winter, were suited to different surfaces or dried faster.

Books of secrets frequently include formulas for portable instant inks and for cheap inks. The latter varieties had particular significance for Sir Hugh Plat (see p.55), developing recipes in times of terrible famine and hardship. He improved low quality inks by adding 'liquors' – small amounts of fine ink made up from expensive formulas.

Ink recipe (translated opposite) from Ugo da Carpi, *Thesauro de scrittori*, 3rd edition (Rome, 1535). With slight changes, it repeats a formula contained in the first printed writing-book, the *Theorica et pratica … de modo scribendi* (*Theory and Practice of Writing*) (Venice, 1514), by the Sienese noble and writing-master Sigismondo Fanti. That recipe was also copied in two writing-books both cut by Eustachio Celebrino, the expanded 2nd edition of Giovanni Antonio Tagliente's *Lo presente libro insegna la vera arte …* (*This Book Teaches the True Art [of Writing]*) (1524) and Arrighi's *Il modo di temperare le penne* (*How to Cut Quills*) (1523/4).

V&A/NAL: Special Collections, 87.C.74, f.44v

PRINTING INK

To make printing ink

PRINTERS' INK IS MADE SOLELY WITH THE SMOKE OF ROSIN [lampblack] and is tempered with liquid varnish. It must be seethed a little to make it more liquid and [or] harder. In winter, it needs to be more liquid than in summer. To make it flow more, add more linseed or walnut oil. To thicken, add less oil and more smoke and let it boil for longer. The thicker it is, the more beautiful, clean, black and glossy the letters are. However you make it, it must be mixed thoroughly. To print in red, add perfectly ground vermilion in place of the said smoke.

✳ ✳ ✳ ✳ ✳ ✳ ✳ ✳ ✳
✳ ✳ ✳ ✳ ✳ ✳
✳ ✳ ✳
✳

Jost Amman, woodcut depicting *Der Buchdrücker* (*The Printer*), from *Eygentliche Beschreibung aller Stände* (*The Book of Trades*) by Hans Sachs. Ink on paper, Germany (Frankfurt am Main), 1568. In this illustration of a printer's workshop a pressman is applying the sticky ink to the forme with two inking balls, usually made of stuffed leather with wooden handles. The book depicts contemporary professions, trades and crafts, each illustrated by a detailed woodcut and a poem in rhyming couplets. It presents a microcosm of manufacturing and society in 16th-century Nuremberg, and celebrates the virtues of the mechanical arts.

V&A/NAL: 86.D.46

IMPRESSIO LIBRORVM.
Poteſt vt vna vox capi aure plurima: Linunt ita vna ſcripta mille paginas.
5.

Jan van der Straet (Stradanus), *Impressio librorum* (*Book printing*). Engraving from the series *Nova Reperta* (*New Discoveries*), first published in Antwerp, late 16th century, celebrating the wonders of the new age, such as the invention of gunpowder, the compass, the discovery of America, even distilling and the raising of silkworms. In the foreground a man selects letters for his composing stick following a manuscript pinned to the wall, whilst to the right the printing press is being pulled.

V&A: 93.H.963

The exact composition of early printing ink remains unknown. This was a trade secret that was not disclosed since it was commercially sensitive. The rough description opposite from the *Secreti del reverendo donno Alessio Piemontese* (*The Secrets of Don Alessio Piemontese*) (Venice, 1555) is probably reliable as its presumed author, Gerolamo Ruscelli, did briefly have a printing business.

Further tantalizing hints are contained in other mid-sixteenth-century sources. The second edition of Vannoccio Biringuccio's *La Pirotechnia* (*The Art of Fire*) (Venice, 1550) states that books are printed using 'an ink made up of soot of linseed oil or resin that has been mixed with liquid varnish and well incorporated'. Leonardo Fioravanti (see p.73) in his *Compendio dei secreti rationali* (*Compendium of Rational Secrets*) (Venice, 1564) goes into further detail. An ounce of lampblack should be added to every pound of liquid varnish. The mixture, thoroughly combined, should be boiled on a low heat. An Inquisition trial in Salamanca even reveals that 'when they make the varnish the (print) workers eat the linseed oil spread on toast, and their hands black with varnish, eat the bread covered with ink'.

Extensive research has been directed towards the first inks produced by Johann Gutenberg, acclaimed for their quality. Low-intensity beams of protons were fired at a copy of the 42-line Bible, the first real book printed with movable type. The X-rays emitted as the protons collided with the atoms in the ink were detected and analysed. Gutenberg's ink was found to be unusually rich in compounds of lead and copper.

Lodovico Guicciardini described the printing house of Christophe Plantin in 1581 as unsurpassed in Europe. In *La première et la seconde partie des dialogues françois pour les jeunes enfants* (*First and Second Part of the Dialogues for Young Children in French*) (Antwerp, 1567), Plantin refers to printing ink as made from 'turpentine, oil and lampblack'. His operation was on an industrial scale: the accounts reveal that printing ink was not produced in-house, but was bought in Antwerp in huge quantities from specialist firms of ink makers (*ancriers, faiseurs d'encre*).

How to Cut Quills

SCRAPE AWAY THE GREASY MEMBRANE ON TOP WITH THE BACK of the penknife. Then make the first [scooping] cut on the same side as the groove [the underside of the barrel] to a length you see fit. Next form with two further cuts into an elegant shape resembling a sparrow-hawk's beak (as you see in the illustration). Both sides of the 'ploughshare' (as we call the part below the first cut) should be made with two symmetrical cuts, as already explained. Next, place on your thumbnail (on which you can have a thimble if you wish), trim it a little and cut the point according to the size of letter you want. Note that for the chancery hand it should be cut lame [obliquely] so the right side of the nib resting on your thumbnail is slightly shorter than the left [...] Next make a small slit in the nib with the tip of your penknife and lightly scrape the sides to remove any roughness [...]

Kept clean as stated above [never allow the tip to dry out][...] it will write excellently.

✳ ✳ ✳ ✳ ✳ ✳ ✳ ✳ ✳
✳ ✳ ✳ ✳ ✳ ✳ ✳
✳ ✳ ✳ ✳
✳

Title page with author portrait from Giovambattista Palatino, *Libro nuovo d'imparare a scrivere* (Rome, 1540).

V&A/NAL: RC.G.35

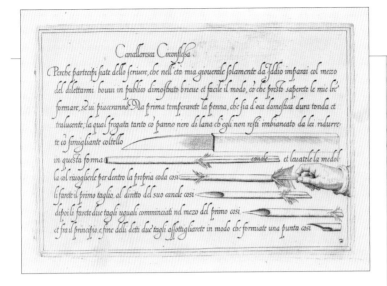

For his second book, *Il modo di temperare le penne* (*How to Cut Quills*), Ludovico Arrighi joined forces with another first-rate engraver, Eustachio Celebrino (see p.11). Exactly when remains a mystery; but Celebrino was working on a rival publication for another writing-master, the Venetian Giovanni Antonio Tagliente, before November 1524. With plagiarism rife and copying older material into 'new' works an accepted practice, it is no surprise that the same passage outlining the five qualities of a good quill shows up in certain editions of both books. Quills should be large, hard, round, narrow and taken from the right wing. Best of all were those taken from a domestic goose. Both writers provide a step-by-step guide to sharpening quills (as do earlier texts by Sigismondo Fanti and Cennino Cennini).

A generation later, their instructions were attacked in print by Giovambattista Palatino in a new manifesto, the *Libro nuovo d'imparare a scrivere tutte sorte lettere* (*New Book for Learning to Write*) (Rome, 1540), 'the most celebrated and most often reprinted of all the Italian writing manuals'. The old directions were convoluted, confusing, difficult to understand. His new rules (reproduced opposite) would be their antithesis. Palatino, who had acquired Roman citizenship only two years previously, was one of the founding members of the *Accademia dello Sdegno* (Academy of the Disdainful). So too was Girolamo Ruscelli, author of the most famous book of secrets of them all, under the pseudonym of Alessio Piemontese. The *Libro nuovo* reflects the interests of this intellectual discussion group, under the patronage of the young Cardinal Alessandro Farnese. One of the book's innovations was a 'short, useful treatise on ciphers'. Palatino describes Ruscelli as an expert cryptographer, from whom he learnt 'several useful and beautiful secrets' for invisible writing on glass. Significantly, the Brescian noble Giovan Battista Bellaso also dedicated his short booklet *La cifra* (*The Cipher*) (Venice, 1553) to Ruscelli, and his *Il vero modo di scrivere in cifra, con facilita, prestezza et securezza* (*The True Method of Writing in Cipher …*) (Brescia, 1564) to Farnese.

The revolution in visual communication in the Renaissance had a profound effect on the use of illustrations as powerful tools for information and communication, notably in the fields of natural history and anatomy. The use of graphics in calligraphy manuals was self-evident, above all for writing specimens. But their value in conveying the complex cutting process precisely and quickly was clearly not lost on Palatino (nor on Arrighi, who included a five-stage diagram of a cut quill).

The example of Palatino's *Libro nuovo* demonstrates that oral, visual and printed media all interacted in the transmission of secrets. Rather than looking at secrets within print culture alone, it makes more sense to study them within a larger multimedia system.

Marbled Paper

A way of colouring paper in a Turkish manner

IMMERSE GUM TRAGACANTH IN VERY PURE WATER FOR THREE DAYS until it dissolves into a white solution. Then strain and pour into a trough [the size of a full sheet of paper] [...] two to three fingers deep. Watch carefully that its consistency is neither thicker nor thinner than water [...] Light colours are most suitable: red lake, indigo for sky-blue, orpiment for yellow and lead white [...] Dissolve separately in water some egg white, ox gall and petroleum [...] With a brush first sprinkle the preparation on the solution. Observe the drops form fully complete circles on the surface of the paper. If they do not hold together, pour in some new ox gall and mix until the desired end is attained. The colours themselves are sprinkled separately in no exact order.

The method of designing a plume on paper

WITH A REED DRAW IN ONE DIRECTION ACROSS THE TROUGH and from side to side, cutting all the drops of colour and elongating them. You may draw a comb with equally spaced teeth [and the depth of the trough] along its length and breadth. Drawing the colours across and cutting them perpendicularly forms leaves and plumes.

Marbled paper from the friendship book of Wolfgang Leutkauff. This album includes 141 decorated papers (including 34 types of marbled paper on 46 sheets).

V&A/NAL: MSL/1889/1392. f.80r

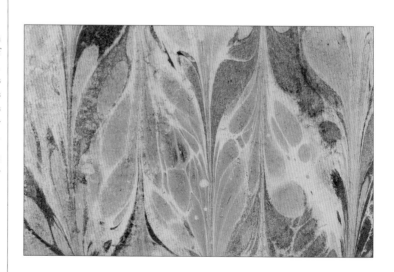

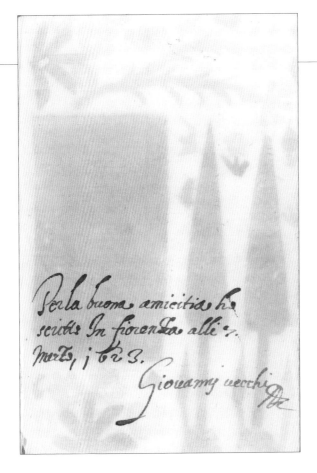

Silhouette paper from
the friendship book of
Wolfgang Leutkauff.

V&A/NAL:
MSL/1889/1392. f.116r

Friendship books (*alba amicorum*) were the early modern equivalents of autograph albums or Facebook. They originated amongst students and scholars from Germany and the Low Countries who collected signatures and dedications from those they met on their travels. By 1558, as the fashion spread, finely bound blank albums became available. It was customary for students from noble families to have their contributions embellished by coats of arms painted by skilled painters at their own expense.

By the mid-1570s, European travellers to the Near East were adding Turkish decorated papers – marbled paper (*abri*), silhouette paper and sprinkled paper – to their albums. These were high-cost items and a street in Istanbul is known to have specialized in their sale. The marbled and silhouette papers illustrated here come from a friendship book in the National Art Library belonging to the Viennese Wolfgang Leutkauff who visited Italy, Istanbul, Adrianople and Belgrade between 1616 and 1632.

The techniques of marbling were closely guarded. In Europe, Geerard ter Brugghen only published the first instructions in Amsterdam in 1616. However, marbled paper was produced in southern Germany from before 1604. The formula above comes from the *Ars magna lucis et umbrae* (*Great Art of Light and Shadow*) (1646), a work on light and optics, by the Jesuit polymath Athanasius Kircher (1602–80), suggested for the title of 'the last man who knew everything'.

Silhouette paper (like marbling, a technique inherited from Iran) was produced from designs created using thin leather cutouts, soaked in coloured dyes. These were then printed between folded sheets of paper. The paper was brushed with a solution of *aher* (alum and beaten egg whites) and matt-finished with a polishing stone. This additional treatment added to its price.

Sources

Anon., *Opera nuoua intitolata Dificio de ricette, nella quale si contengono tre utilissimi ricettari* (Venice, 1525)

Anon., Descriptions for making braided strings (England, 1625–50), manuscript. V&A/NAL: T.313-1960

Bardi family recipe book (Florence, 16th century), manuscript. Florence, Archivio di Stato, Carte Bardi, II serie n.40, part published by Antonio Torresi, *Il Ricettario Bardi: cosmesi e tecnica artistica nella Firenze medicea* (Ferrara, 1994)

Vannoccio Biringuccio, *De la pirotechnia. Libri .X. Dove ampiamente si tratta non solo di ogni sorte & diuersita di miniere, ma anchora quanto si ricerca intorno à la prattica di quelle cose di quel che si appartiene à l'arte de la fusione ouer gitto de metalli come d'ogni altra cosa simile à questa* (Venice, 1540)

Ugo da Carpi, *Thesauro de scrittori. Opera artificiosa laquale con grandissima arte, si per pratica come per geometria insegna a scriuere diuerse sorte littere … intagliata per Ugo da Carpi* (Rome, 1525)

Cennino Cennini, *Il libro dell'arte* (Florence, between 1396 and 1427), manuscript. Florence, Biblioteca Mediceo-Laurenziana: MS 23 and Biblioteca Riccardiana: MS 2190. Translated by Daniel V. Thompson, Jr (New Haven, Conn., 1933)

Vincenzo Cervio, *Il Trinciante* (Venice, 1583)

Isabella Cortese, *I secreti de la signora Isabella Cortese ne' quali si contengono cose minerali, medicinali, arteficiose, et alchimiche, et molte de l'arte profumatoria. Appartenenti a ogni gran signora, con privilegio* (Venice, 1561)

Oswald Croll, *Basilica chymica, continens philosophicam propria laborum experientia confirmatam descriptionem et usum remediorum chymicorum selectissimorum è lumine gratiae & naturae desumptorum* (Frankfurt, 1609)

Leonardo Fioravanti, *Del compendio dei secreti rationali, dell'eccell. medico & cirugico m. Leonardo Fiorauanti bolognese, libri cinque* (Venice, 1564)

Leonardo Fioravanti, *Della fisica dell'eccellente dottore et cauialiero. M. Leonardo Fiorauanti Bolognese. Diuisa in libri quattro* (Venice, 1582)

Tomaso da Francolino, [L'Ortolano], *Tesoro di secreti naturali* (Rome, Venice, Milan, Siena, Bologna, Pesaro, Macerata, 1617)

Athanasius Kircher, *Ars magna lucis et umbrae* (Rome, 1646)

Wolfgang Leutkauff, *Album amicorum*, 1616-1632. Album composed of plain and coloured paper, including 141 decorated leaves, 46 marbled, some touched with gold. V&A/NAL: MSL/1889/1392

Gabrielle Magino, *Dialoghi di M. Magino Gabrielli hebreo venetiano sopra l'utili sue inuentioni circa la seta. Ne' quali anche si dimostrano in vaghe figure historiati tutti gl'essercitij, & instrumenti, che nell'arte della seta si ricercano* (Rome, 1588)

Giovanni Marinello, *Gli ornamenti delle donne, tratti dalle scritture d'una reina Greca per m. Giovanni Marinello […] Opera utile, & necessaria ad ogni gentile persona* (Venice, 1562)

Giovanni Marinello, *Delle medicine partenenti all' infermità delle donne scritte per m. Giovanni Marinello, & divise in tre libri* (Venice, 1563)

Leonard Mascall, *A profitable boke declaring dyuers approoued remedies, to take out spottes and staines, in silkes, veluets, linnnen, and woollen clothes* (London, 1583)

Giovan Batista Nardi, *Chirurgia e segreti diversi* (*c*.1585), Florence: Biblioteca Nazionale Centrale, Codice Magliabechiana gia Palatino, Cl. XV, n.142, published by Giovanni Battista Baldelli-Boni in 1827 and in Galeazzo Cora and A. Fanfani, *La porcellana dei Medici* (Milan, 1986)

Antonio Neri, *L'arte vetraria distinta in libri sette del r. p. Antonio Neri fiorentino. Ne quali si scoprono, effetti marauigliosi, & insegnano segreti bellissimi, del vetro nel fuoco & altre cose curiose* (Florence, 1612)

Giovambattista Palatino, *Libro nuovo d'imparare a scrivere tutte sorte lettere* (Rome, 1540)

Bernard Palissy, *Discours admirables, de la nature des eaux et fonteines, tant naturelles qu'artificielles, des metaux … du feu et des emaux* (Paris, 1580)

Cipriano Piccolpasso, *I tre libri dell'arte del vasaio*, (Castel Durante, 1556–9), manuscript. V&A/NAL: MSL/1861/7446. Facsimile edition translated by Ronald Lightbown and Alan Caiger-Smith (London, 1980)

Alessio Piemontese: *see* Girolamo Ruscelli

Sir Hugh Plat, *The Jewell House of Art and Nature. Conteining divers rare and profitable inventions, together with sundry new experimentes in the art of husbandry, distillation and moulding* (London, 1594)

Stefano Rosselli, *Segreti diversi*, (Florence, 1569–88), manuscript. Florence, Biblioteca Mediceo-Laurenziana: MS Antinori 151

Timoteo Rossello, *Della summa de' secreti universali in ogni materia parte prima* (Venice, 1559)

Giovanventura Rosetti, *Notandissimi secreti de l'arte profumatoria: a fare ogli, acque, paste, balle, moscardini, uccelletti, paternostri, e tutta l'arte intiera, come si ricerca cosi ne la citta di Napoli del Reame, come in Roma, e quiui in la citta di Vinegia nuouamente impressi* (Venice, 1555)

Giovanventura Rosetti, *Plichto de l'arte de tentori che insegna tenger panni telle banbasi et sede si per larthe magiore come per la commune* (Venice, 1548). Facsimile edition translated by Sidney M. Edelstein (Boston, Mass., 1969)

[Girolamo Ruscelli], *Secreti del reverendo donno Alessio Piemontese. Nuovamente posti in luce. Opera utile, et necessaria universalmente à ciascuno* (Venice, 1555)

[Girolamo Ruscelli], *Secreti di don Alessio Piemontese nuouamente stampati. Con vna bellissima aggiunta de secreti hauti da un religioso pratichissimo, & eccellente, & esperimentati* (Lucca, 1557)

Hans Sachs, *Eygentliche Beschreibung aller Stände auff Erden: Hoher und Nidriger, Geistlicher und Weltlicher, aller Künsten, Handwerken und Händeln, … Erfundung und gebreuchen … in Teutsche Reimen gefasset* (Frankfurt, 1568)

Pietro Paolo di Carlo Beccuti Scala, *Segreti et ricette diversi* (Florence, *c*.1580). Biblioteca Nazionale Centrale di Firenze: II-163

Bartolomeo Scappi, *Opera … divisa in sei libri* (Venice, 1570); English translation by Terence Scully (Toronto, 2009)

Giovanni Antonio Tagliente, *Opera di Giovanni Antonio Taiente che insegna a scriuere di molte qualita di lettere intitulata Lucidario: Lo presente libro insegna la vera arte delo excellente scriuere de diuerse varie sorti de litere le quali se fano per geometrica ragione* (Venice, *c*.1524)

FURTHER READING

Marta Ajmar-Wollheim and Flora Dennis (eds), *At Home in Renaissance Italy* (exhib. cat., London, 2006)

Ken Albala, *The Banquet: Dining in the Great Courts of Late Renaissance Europe* (Urbana, 2007)

Leonard Amico, *Bernard Palissy: In Search of Earthly Paradise* (Paris and New York, 1996)

Charles Avery and Anthony Radcliffe (eds), *Giambologna, 1529–1608: Sculptor to the Medici* (London, 1978)

Andrea Bayer (ed.), *Art and Love in the Renaissance* (New Haven, Conn. and London, 2008)

Lucia Burgio and Bruno Brunetti, 'Lustre ceramics analysis using the MOLAB facilities', *V&A Conservation Journal,* 51 (Autumn 2005)

Peter Burke, *The European Renaissance: Centres and Peripheries* (Oxford, 1998)

Karel Davids, 'Introduction. Craft secrecy in Europe in the Early Modern period: a comparative view', *Early Science and Medicine,* 10:3 (1985), pp. 341–8.

William Eamon, *Science and the Secrets of Nature: Books of Secrets in Medieval and Early Modern Culture* (Princeton, N.J., 2004)

Stephan R. Epstein and Maarten Prak, *Guilds, Innovation, and the European Economy, 1400–1800* (Cambridge, 2008)

Miguel Falomir (ed.), *Tintoretto* (London, 2007)

Sharon Fermor, *The Raphael Tapestry Cartoons: Narrative, Decoration, Design* (London, 1996)

Paula Findlen, *Possessing Nature: Museums, Collecting, and Scientific Culture in Early Modern Italy* (Berkeley, 1994)

Margaret Gallucci and Paolo L. Rossi (eds), *Benvenuto Cellini: Sculptor, Goldsmith, Writer* (Cambridge, 2004)

David Gentilcore, *Medical Charlatanism in Early Modern Italy* (Oxford, 2006)

Deborah Harkness, *The Jewel House: Elizabethan London and the Scientific Revolution* (New Haven, Conn. and London, 2007)

David Jenkins (ed.), *The Cambridge History of Western Textiles,* Vol. I (Cambridge, 2002)

Reino Liefkes (ed.), *Glass* (London, 1997)

Pamela O. Long, *Openness, Secrecy, Authorship: Technical Arts and the Culture of Knowledge from Antiquity to the Renaissance* (Baltimore, 2001)

Rosamond Mack, *Bazaar to Piazza: Islamic Trade and Italian Art, 1300–1600* (Berkeley and London, 2002)

Luca Molà, *The Silk Industry of Renaissance Venice* (Baltimore, 2000)

Stanley Morrison, *Early Italian Writing Books: Renaissance to Baroque* (London, 1990)

Jacqueline Musacchio, *The Art and Ritual of Childbirth in Renaissance Italy* (New Haven, Conn. and London, 1999)

Jacqueline Musacchio, *Art, Marriage, and Family in the Florentine Renaissance Palace* (New Haven, Conn. and London, 2008)

Tara Nummedal, *Alchemy and Authority in the Holy Roman Empire* (Chicago, 2007)

Jutta-Annette Page (ed.), *Beyond Venice: Glass in Venetian Style, 1500–1750* (Corning, N.Y., 2004)

Alisha Rankin, 'Becoming an expert practitioner: court experimentalism and the medical skills of Anna of Saxony (1532–1585)', *Isis*, 98:1 (2007), pp.23–53.

Brian Richardson, *Printing, Writers and Readers in Renaissance Italy* (Cambridge, 1999)

Pamela H. Smith, 'In a sixteenth-century goldsmith's workshop', in Lissa Roberts, Simon Schaffer, Peter Dear (eds), *The Mindful Hand: Inquiry and Invention from the Late Renaissance to Early Industrialisation* (Amsterdam, 2007)

Pamela H. Smith and Benjamin Schmidt, *Making Knowledge in Early Modern Europe: Practices, Objects, and Texts, 1400–1800* (Chicago, 2008)

Luke Syson and Dora Thornton, *Objects of Virtue: Art in Renaissance Italy* (London, 2001)

Marjorie Trusted (ed.), *The Making of Sculpture: The Materials and Techniques of European Sculpture* (London, 2007)

Wendy Wall, *Staging Domesticity: Household Work and English Identity in Early Modern Drama* (Cambridge, 2002)

Evelyn Welch, *Shopping in the Renaissance: Consumer Cultures in Italy 1400–1600* (New Haven, 2005)

Steve Wharton, 'What you see is what you get: colour in Italian Renaissance istoriato ware', *Renaissance Quarterly*, 19:5 (2005), pp.592–603.

Timothy Wilson, *Ceramic Art of the Italian Renaissance* (London, 1987)

Richard J. Wolfe, *Marbled Paper: Its History, Techniques, and Patterns* (Philadelphia, 1990)

INDEX

RENAISSANCE
SECRETS
RECIPES & FORMVLAS